GRANTA

THE FAMILY

37

Editor: Bill Buford
Deputy Editor: Tim Adams
Managing Editor: Ursula Doyle
Editorial Assistant: Robert McSweeney
Contributing Editor: Lucretia Stewart

Managing Director: Derek Johns
Financial Controller: Geoffrey Gordon

Picture Editor: Alice Rose George
Design: Chris Hyde
Executive Editor: Pete de Bolla
US Associate Publisher: Anne Kinard, Granta, 250 West 57th Street, Suite 1316, New York, NY 10107.

Editorial and Subscription Correspondence: Granta, 2–3 Hanover Yard, Noel Road, Islington, London N1 8BE. Telephone: (071) 704 9776. Fax: (071) 704 0474. Subscriptions: (071) 837 7765.
A one-year subscription (four issues) is £19.95 in Britain, £25.95 for the rest of Europe, and £31.95 for the rest of the world.
All manuscripts are welcome but must be accompanied by a stamped, self-addressed envelope or they cannot be returned.

Granta is printed in the United States of America. The paper used in this publication meets the minimum requirements of American National Standard for Information Sciences—Permanence of Paper for Printed Library Materials, ANSI Z39.48-1984. ∞

Cover by Senate
'They fuck you up' is taken from 'This Be The Verse' by Philip Larkin, in *High Windows* published by The Marvell Press and Faber and Faber.

Granta 37, Autumn 1991

ISBN 0-14-015207-5

A marvellous novel, set in a small farming community, outside Bakersfield, California. It interweaves the lives of seven women of varying ages and backgrounds who meet weekly at the quilting club.

An astonishing mature debut, and a work already being compared to Amy Tan's *The Joy Luck Club*.

'An impressive feat . . . an affirmation of the strength and power of individual lives, and the way they cannot help fitting together'
New York Times Book Review

Hardback   UK Publication date 12 July 1991

Sahka and Kolka are orphaned identical twins. During the second world war they struggle for survival in a Moscow orphanage where food is scarce and love and attention non-existent. They rely on each other completely; they are inseparable.

Based on the author's own experiences, and written in great secrecy, this courageous novel has now been heralded in Russia as a great literary event.

Hardback   UK Publication date 9 August 1991

P.J. O'Rourke sets out to examine and explain every aspect of government, making it at the same time wholly intelligible and hilariously funny.

Among the topics he dissects are *The Three Branches of Government: Money, Television and Bullshit* and *Why God is a Republican and Santa Claus is a Democrat*.

'The funniest American writer I have read since Thurber'
Tom Sharpe

Hardback   UK Publication date 6 September 1991

CONTENTS

MIKAL GILMORE
FAMILY ALBUM

I am the brother of a man who murdered innocent men. His name was Gary Gilmore. After his conviction and sentencing, he campaigned to end his own life, and in January 1977 he was shot to death by a firing-squad in Draper, Utah. It was the first execution in America in over a decade.

Many people know this part of the Gary Gilmore story. It was an international news item in 1976 and 1977, and it became the subject of a popular novel and television film. What is less well known, what has never been documented, is the origin of Gary's violence—the history of my family. It isn't a comforting story to tell, nor has it been an easy legacy to live with. Over the years, many people have judged me by my brother's actions as if in coming from a family that yielded a murderer I must be formed by the same causes, the same sins, must by my brother's actions be responsible for the violence that resulted, and bear the mark of a frightening and shameful heritage. It's as if there is guilt in the fact of the blood-line itself. Maybe there is.

M ormon Utah in the early twentieth century was a nation within a nation. The Mormons had been persecuted horribly in the early nineteenth century. They had been driven across the country to the western desert. They had come to believe in violence, not just for protection, but for punishing abuses and betrayals, for vengeance. The early Mormons formed vendetta squads—such as the bloody Sons of Dan—to deal with enemies and traitors.

The Mormons developed a doctrine of blood atonement: if you took life, then you must lose your own (a prescription never applied to the Church's official assassins). They believed in capital punishment. The bloodier the execution, the better. Atoning for murder required a sacrifice: there should be ritual, blood, witnesses. Mormons favoured death by firing-squad or by hanging; these were—and today remain—the only options available to the condemned in Mormon law. Hangings were public. The gallows were placed in meadows or valleys, and

Opposite: Frank and Bessie Gilmore with (from the left) Frank Jr, Gary and Gaylen, 1949.

Mormons brought their families to watch.

Bessie Gilmore was born Bessie Brown in 1913, the fourth of nine children, in the strict Mormon community of Provo, Utah. She often told us that she remembered being loaded by her father into the family wagon one winter morning, along with her brothers and sisters, and being driven in darkness to a hanging ceremony. She watched the man being led up the stairs to the noose and the executioner. She would not watch the hanging but shut her eyes tight and buried her face in her father's side. She heard the trapdoor crack open, then a horrible snapping sound as the man's weight hit the end of the rope's length and his head was yanked loose from his body. She heard cheers and applause. On moving away from the site, she turned back and saw the man's body dangling and swaying. Men around her were holding the hands of their children, pointing at the corpse, admonishing their brood to remember the moment and the lesson.

Bessie Brown remembered. The event haunted and terrified her for the rest of her life. She began to hate her own people—or at least the beliefs that would allow them to participate in hanging. When I was a child, and we were living in Portland, Oregon, she anxiously followed the news of impending executions. She wrote letters to the governor, arguing against the death penalty on moral grounds, asking the state to commute the condemned person's sentence. She asked me, or any of my brothers who might be around, to join her at the dining table and write our own letters to the governor. She explained that these were the only killings we *knew* were going to occur and the only killings we could prevent.

She called the men who had arranged the public hangings the dead-makers. Mormon law had made it permissible for those watching to enjoy the deaths. She imagined that the executions unleashed the demons of the hanged murderers—demons that flew from the gaping mouths of the men as their necks snapped and their souls departed, and then, once loose, were free to find new victims and haunt the witnesses to the deaths.

When she got older, Bessie began to drink and smoke—two habits forbidden to Mormons—and to flirt with boys. She wore pretty dresses to the Church dances and stayed out all night. One morning, sneaking back home, her father caught her. He called her terrible names and beat her. She ran away; her parents found her living in San Francisco; they dragged her home. A few months later, she ran away again.

Eventually, she ran away for good. One afternoon in Salt Lake City she was visiting some girl-friends at one of the city's best hotels when she saw a beautiful man stroll into the lobby. Frank Gilmore was dressed in a fine suit and wore spats and carried a cane. She was dazzled. He was the most debonair person she had ever seen. She met him; he charmed her. He was not a Mormon.

My father was born in the late 1890s and grew up among spiritualists, vaudevillians and circus performers. His mother Fay La Foe had worked for many years as a medium, holding seances, telling fortunes, acting as a broker between the living and the dead. It was rumoured that in her younger days she had an affair with an up-and-coming magician, Erich Weiss—later famous as Harry Houdini. One of the family legends was that my father was their offspring, that he was Houdini's bastard son. According to my mother, my father's real name was Francis Weiss. She did not know where the name Gilmore came from. It was one of the many surnames he used during his life.

Frank Gilmore was a ladies' man. He was handsome and intelligent, he dressed splendidly and told captivating stories. He had been a stunt man for the actor Harry Carey and others in the silent film era, and for years worked as a tightwire-walking clown in the Barnum and Bailey Circus under the name of Laffo, until a long fall without a net left him with a severely broken leg and injured back. He claimed that he had been a drinking buddy of Frank James and Buffalo Bill, in the Wild West's closing days. The only item of self-mythology he never vaunted was his possible relation to Harry Houdini; it was his mother who made that boast, to his irritation. He did not want to be the son of a man whom he would never know.

Frank Gilmore was twenty years older than my mother. He

was married, with two children, when she met him. But she wanted to marry him. Frank Gilmore left his wife and in 1939 was married to Bessie Brown in a service conducted by his mother, who had a clergyman's licence in the Spiritualist Church. Her father was outraged and ashamed.

Whatever enjoyment Frank and Bessie may have had, it did not last long. By the time Frank Jr was born, my father was sullen and drinking heavily, and he and my mother bickered about money, family and religion constantly. My mother tried to keep pace with his drinking, making the nightly rounds of taverns with him as a way of forging a truce, but when she became pregnant again, she stopped drinking.

My father did not want a second child. He claimed the child was not his. He demanded that my mother have an abortion. One night, drunk, he beat her. He beat her again a few nights later. She left with Frank Jr and went to her father's farm. My father brought her back. They made a peace. Gary was born in 1941. My father neglected his second son; over the years, the disregard would turn to mutual hatred.

Pictures in the family scrap-book show my father with his children. I have only one photograph of him and Gary together. Gary is wearing a sailor's cap. He has his arms wrapped tightly around my father's neck, his head bent towards him, a look of broken need on his face. It is heart-breaking to look at this picture—not just for the look on Gary's face, the look that was the stamp of his future, but also for my father's expression: pulling away from my brother's cheek, he is wearing a look of distaste.

When my brother Gaylen was born in the mid forties, my father turned all his love on his new, beautiful brown-eyed son. Gary takes on a harder aspect in the pictures around this time. He was beginning to keep a greater distance from the rest of the family. Six years later, my father turned his love from Gaylen to me. You don't see Gary in the family pictures after that.

Gary had nightmares. It was always the same dream: he was being beheaded.

In 1953, Gary was arrested for breaking windows. He was

sent to a juvenile detention home for ten months, where he saw young men raped and beaten. Two years later, at age fourteen, he was arrested for car theft and sentenced to eighteen months in jail. I was four years old.

When I was growing up I did not feel accepted by, or close to, my brothers. By the time I was four or five, they had begun to find life and adventure outside the home. Frank, Gary and Gaylen signified the teenage rebellion of the fifties for me. They wore their hair in greasy pompadours and played Elvis Presley and Fats Domino records. They dressed in scarred motorcycle jackets and brutal boots. They smoked cigarettes, drank booze and cough syrup, skipped—and quit—school, and spent their evenings hanging out with girls in tight sweaters, racing souped-up cars along country roads outside Portland, or taking part in gang rumbles. My brothers looked for a forbidden life—the life they had seen exemplified in the crime lore of gangsters and killers. They studied the legends of violence. They knew the stories of John Dillinger, Bonnie and Clyde, and Leopold and Loeb; mulled over the meanings of the lives and executions of Barbara Graham, Bruno Hauptmann, Sacco and Vanzetti, the Rosenbergs; thrilled to the pleading of criminal lawyers like Clarence Darrow and Jerry Giesler. They brought home books about condemned men and women, and read them avidly.

I remember loving my brothers fiercely, wanting to be a part of their late-night activities and to share in their laughter and friendship. I also remember being frightened of them. They looked deadly, beyond love, destined to hurt the world around them.

One hot summer afternoon, I was sitting in the living-room watching television when my brother Gaylen walked through the front door. He was bare-chested and covered with blood. He had tried to join a local gang. For the initiation, the gang-lord had stripped him and tied him up, then shot him repeatedly with a pellet rifle. Gaylen sat in a chair at the kitchen table as my mother washed the blood from him and picked the pellets from his arms and chest. She cried and talked about calling the police, but Gaylen made her promise that she wouldn't.

15

Mikal Gilmore, 1959.

Gary came home from reform school for a brief Christmas visit. On Christmas night I was sitting in my room, playing with the day's haul of presents, when Gary wandered in. 'Hey Mike, how you doing?' he asked, taking a seat on my bed. 'Think I'll just join you while I have a little Christmas cheer.' He had a six-pack of beer with him and was speaking in a bleary drawl. 'Look partner, I want to have a talk with you.' I think it was the first companionable statement he ever made to me. I never expected the intimacy that followed and could not really fathom it at such a young age. Sitting on the end of my bed, sipping at his Christmas beer, Gary described a harsh, private world and told me horrible, transfixing stories: about the boys he knew in the detention halls, reform schools and county farms where he now spent most of his time; about the bad boys who had taught him the merciless codes of his new life; and about the soft boys who did not have what it took to survive that life. He said he had shared a cell with one of the soft boys, who cried at night, wanting to disappear into nothing, while Gary held him in his arms until the boy finally fell into sleep, sobbing.

Then Gary gave me some advice. 'You have to learn to be hard. You have to learn to take things and feel nothing about them: no pain, no anger, nothing. And you have to realize, if anybody wants to beat you up, even if they want to hold you down and kick you, you have to let them. You can't fight back. You *shouldn't* fight back. Just lie down in front of them and let them beat you, let them kick you. Lie there and let them do it. It is the only way you will survive. If you don't give in to them, they will kill you.'

He set aside his beer and cupped my face in his hands. 'You have to remember this, Mike,' he said. 'Promise me. Promise me you'll be a man. Promise me you'll let them beat you.' We sat there on that winter night, staring at each other, my face in his hands, and as Gary asked me to promise to take my beatings, his bloodshot eyes began to cry. It was the first time I had seen him shed tears.

I promised: Yes, I'll let them kick me. But I was afraid— afraid of betraying Gary's plea.

My father had taken his love from everybody else in the family and came to favour only me with it. This was another reason I felt apart from my brothers and I have never been comfortable admitting it. I was held up to them as the example of worth and goodness that they were not. Before I was born, Gaylen had been the favoured one. After I arrived, my father shunned Gaylen, made fun of him, called him fat, hit him, accused him of heading towards Gary's criminal life—which he accordingly did. My father never brutalized me, as he had brutalized Gary and Gaylen. Maybe he saw me as his last chance

17

at successful love.

I remember my father finishing one tirade by taking Gaylen's pearl-handled, nickel-plated toy revolver, one of Gaylen's favourite possessions, and giving it to me. A day or two later, after my father left town on business, Gaylen dragged all my toys into the side yard and locked me in the house. I watched out of the dining-room window as he smashed toy after toy with an axe. He tossed the shattered heap of plastic in the trash can. When he came back in, he was crying. 'Someday,' he said in a voice thick with pain, 'he'll hate you too.'

Then there was the incident on Christmas Day.

I don't remember how it started, but my father and Gary became embroiled in an ugly confrontation. Each tested the other's toughness. Then they threatened to kill each other. My mother pleaded with them to stop, but the moment was too tense. Gaylen stepped in and asked my father to leave Gary alone. My father—already an old man, but still amazingly strong—made a fist and punched Gaylen in the stomach. I have never forgotten the awfulness of that blow. Gaylen doubled over in pain, and Gary went over to help him. My father grabbed me and said that we were leaving and would spend Christmas in a hotel. I did not want to go, and I said so. 'Don't *you* turn against me too,' he said, and the look of rage and hurt on his face was enough to make me go with him. I was afraid of what he might do to us all if I stayed.

My mother begged my father to remain, to apologize to Gaylen and Gary and try to repair the Christmas, or at least to let me spend the holiday with my brothers. My father would hear none of it. As he and I were in the car, pulling out of the driveway, I looked up at my mother and brothers, who were gathered on the porch, watching us leave. I could tell from the way my brothers were looking at me that they would never forgive me, would never let me into their fraternity.

I felt like a traitor. I wanted to join my brothers—to be standing with them on the porch, watching as the source of their hurt left them—but I knew I never could. I was eight, maybe nine, years old.

The Gilmore brothers, 1959.

In 1960, my family moved from the semi-rural, semi-industrial outskirts of Portland to an upper middle class area nearby, known as Milwaukie. My father had settled down, as much as he knew how to. He had become a self-styled publishing entrepreneur: he compiled the numerous residential and business building codes for the areas of Seattle, Tacoma and Portland, and published them in seasonal manuals in which he sold advertising spaces to local architects and contractors. It proved a lucrative business. We bought a big four-bedroom house with a tear-drop shaped driveway, perched at the top of a hill that afforded a remarkable view of the entire stretch of the Willamette Valley. On clear days, you could view the fast-changing, oddly lopsided skyline of downtown Portland.

My mother saw the relocation as a new start. This was the home she had always wanted, she said, and she set about landscaping the yard with elaborately patterned flower gardens and filling the house with fine furniture imported from Europe and Japan. I think she hoped that a new, better home would rehabilitate the family, give my wayward brothers new pride and win back my father's faith and support for his sons.

19

But Gary was drinking and popping pills. He began hanging out with the friends he had met in jail. He brought home guns. But he proved more a fearless crook than a clever one; he was arrested often, and each new sentence stretched longer than the one before. He had lived most of his adolescence and young adulthood in Oregon's city and county jails and had acquired a reputation as a hard-ass—somebody the other prisoners were not likely to go up against and the jailers would watch warily. He spent over half his jail time in isolation, for defying the institution's rules or for provoking or hitting guards. Many times he found himself in the jail hospital, following beatings by guards. He escaped twice—once by jumping from a second storey window at a pre-trial hearing. It was that escape, I think, that produced his longest free time; he was gone for nearly two years, travelling around the country. One day, we got a call from Texas—the state where Gary had been born. He needed money; he had met a woman he wanted to marry and they were going to have a baby. Reluctantly, my father sent the money. That was the last we ever heard of wife and baby.

Gaylen had his own litany of misdeeds. He was suspended from the local junior high and high schools, and eventually expelled. He stole cars and committed thefts and he drank a good deal more than Gary. By the age of sixteen, Gaylen was a full-fledged alcoholic. In time, he developed his own criminal speciality—forging signatures and writing bad cheques—and, like Gary, spent much of his time in local jails or in flight, skipping bail and violating probation or parole. He joined the navy. He lasted six weeks. After he had gone AWOL five times, the base commanders concluded that Gaylen did not have a military career ahead of him and shipped him back home with an honourable discharge.

If my family sounds like white trash—as many have asserted—well, perhaps it was. Yet we were anomalous white trash. Gary was an artist: I don't mean simply that he could draw well, or that he had pretensions, but that he could draw and paint with remarkable clarity and empathy. The best of his work had the high-lonesome, evocative power of Andrew Wyeth's or Edward Hopper's, though it was more openly haunted and death-obsessed. Gaylen read Poe, Rilke, Nietzsche, Kant, and memorized pages from Shakespeare, Thomas Wolfe and Edwin Arlington Robinson. He also wrote poetry, and it was startling. Like Gary's art, it spoke about being on the outside of life, heading for a self-willed inferno.

Where did this odd mix of raw talent, uncanny intelligence and wasteful ambition come from? Why did their gifts mean so little to my brothers? Why did they prefer a life of crime over a life in art?

I tried to talk to my brothers about their artistic interests, but they didn't want to talk. One afternoon, when Gary and I were sitting around the house, I tried to get him—for the umpteenth time—to show me some basics about drawing. He was drinking cough syrup and laughed in a polite but firm way that announced: *No dice.* I tried to crack Gary's indifference, to tell him I thought he could be a successful artist if he wanted to. Why didn't he make art his life—or at least his vocation? He chased his cough syrup with a swig of beer, then looked at me and smiled. 'You want to learn how to be an artist?' he said. 'Then learn how to eat pussy. Learn that, and it's the only art you'll ever need to learn.'

Gary and Gaylen weren't at home much. I came to know them mainly through their reputations, through the endless parade of grim policemen who came to the door trying to find them, and through the faces and accusations of bail bondsmen and lawyers who arrived looking sympathetic and left disgusted. I knew them through many hours spent in waiting-rooms at city and county jails, where my mother went to visit them, and through the numerous times I accompanied her after midnight to the local police station on Milwaukie's Main Street to bail out another drunken son.

I remember being called into the principal's office while still in grammar school, and being warned that the school would never tolerate my acting as my brothers did; I was told to watch myself, that my brothers had already used years of the school district's good faith and leniency, and that if I was going to be like them, there were other schools I could be sent to. I came to be seen as an extension of my brothers' reputations. Once, I was waiting for a bus in the centre of the small town when a cop pulled over. 'You're one of the Gilmore boys, aren't you? I hope you don't end up like those two. I've seen enough shitheads from your family.' I was walking down the local main highway when a car pulled over and a gang of older teenage boys piled out, surrounding me. 'Are you Gaylen Gilmore's brother?' one of them asked. They shoved me into the car, drove me a few blocks to a deserted lot and took turns punching me in the face. I remembered Gary's advice—'You can't fight back; you *shouldn't* fight back'—and I let them beat me until they were tired. Then they spat on me, got back in their car and left.

I cried all the way back home, and I hated the world. I hated the small town I lived in, its ugly, mean people. For the first time in my life I hated my brothers. I felt that my future would be governed by them, that I would be destined to follow their lives whether I wanted to or not, that I would never know any relief from shame and pain and disappointment. I felt a deep impulse to violence: I wanted to rip the faces off the boys who had beat me up. 'I want to kill them,' I told myself, 'I want to *kill* them'—and as I realized what it was I was saying, and why I was feeling that way, I only hated my world, and my brothers, more.

I've come to understand better why my brothers didn't seem to mind spending so much time in jail: it was preferable to being at home. My parents fought bitterly and often. In the worst fights my father would taunt or insult my mother until, driven by his sure-handed meanness, she would attack him physically. Many times I threw myself between them, trying to stop the fighting, begging them to forgive and love one another (my brothers, when they were home, refused to interfere in these fights; they said the battles had been going on for too many years, and there was no longer any point in becoming involved). Sometimes I succeeded in calming my parents, but the wounds were deep, and my mother would usually end up standing in front of my father, her face contorted in humiliation and fury, swearing that she would knife him in the throat during his sleep for all the pain he had made her feel. My father would fold out the sofa in the living-room and surround it with a fortress of chairs, so he could hear my mother tripping over them if she came to kill him. He would lie down on the sofa to sleep, and he would keep me next to him. Many nights I would lie there, next to my sleeping father, waiting for the sound of footsteps, the creak of floor-boards, the glint of the knife. I would lie there watching the darkness. I would not fall asleep until dawn.

Sometimes, the fights were about me: who would have custody if they divorced or should I stay with my mother or go with my father when he made his trips between Portland and Seattle. My parents insisted that I choose between them. I felt awful no matter what choice I made. This is the way I learned how to love.

The time I spent with my father in Seattle was more peaceful than the time I spent at home in Portland. My father was busy and left me to myself. He didn't care if I stayed home from school for days on end. Because my brothers did not play with me much as a child, I was accustomed to keeping to myself. I filled the day by walking to the zoo, or catching a bus downtown, where I'd hang out in bookstores and movie theatres, or spend hours exploring abandoned Victorian houses in the Queen Anne district.

In the evenings, I sat in the apartment, reading the fantasy fiction of Edgar Rice Burroughs and Jules Verne, the horror stories of Edgar Allan Poe, the epic comic book tales of Carl Barks or the EC crime and horror tales. Then I would huddle close to my father when he arrived home, and we would watch television together until late at night. We liked the westerns and police dramas. We would watch *Maverick, Have Gun Will Travel, Dragnet* or *The Untouchables*, one evening after another, far away from the tumult of the home back in Oregon.

It was during one of these stays in Seattle, in the early months of 1962, that I learned that my father had lung cancer and would die within months. He never knew what was coming. One day he had been old—in his late sixties—but still strong and active; the next he was horribly tired and sick, confined to the bed where he spent the last few months of his life coughing sputum into a bowl. I remember the smell of it, because I lived in the same room with it until the day my father died. It was sickly-sweet, like a spoiled flower. I was surprised that death could be fragrant.

My mother was grief-stricken. She tried to show him tenderness and care, but the years of abuse had taken their toll. As my father slept in the next room, my mother talked about how he had hurt and betrayed her and how she had come to hate him—she hated him more now that he was going to leave her alone with the family, with little money. I had never heard her sound more bitter. I left the room and walked past my father's room and looked in on him. He was sitting on the side of his bed, holding his head in his hands, and when he looked up at me, I saw agony on his face. I went back to my mother and told her that he had overheard what she had said. 'Good,' she replied. 'I wanted him to hear.' Later that night, I found my parents sitting at the kitchen table, holding hands, talking softly. My father was crying, and my mother was petting his hand. I had never seen my parents hold each other's hands before.

Gary stole a car in Portland and drove it up to Seattle to see my father; I think he was hoping for a last chance at reconciliation. On the drive back, Gary was arrested as he crossed the Washington–Oregon border. He was sentenced to a year and a half in the county jail.

Frank Gilmore, Sr died on 30 June 1962. Gary was in Portland's Rocky Butte Jail, and the authorities denied his request to attend the funeral. He tore his cell apart; he smashed a light bulb and slashed his wrists. He was placed in 'the hole'—solitary confinement—on the day of father's funeral. Gary was twenty-one. I was eleven.

I was surprised at how hard my mother and brothers took father's death. I was surprised they loved him enough to cry at all. Or maybe they were crying for the love he had so long withheld, and the reconciliation that would be forever denied them. I was the only one who didn't cry. I don't know why, but I never cried over my father's death—not then, and not now.

Frank Gilmore had not planned for dying. He had not made adequate preparations for his family: there was no will and no money. He left a large house that was still not paid for, and a business that neither my mother nor brothers knew how to operate, though we all tried our hands at it. It wasn't clear who held the copyright on my father's publications, and within a few months, competitors moved in and claimed that he had promised the business to them. Eventually my mother lost control over the publishing; when she did, the family was without solvency and without a financial future. To save the house, and to keep me in school, my mother took a series of menial jobs—working as a crew leader during the summer for children picking berries and beans in local fields, and eventually settling into a job as a waiter's assistant at a local restaurant in downtown Milwaukie. She worked long hours and developed a form of arthritis that proved progressively crippling. She dreamed of the day when she would receive social security payments that were large enough to allow her to quit her job. In time, the work and expenses proved too much. My mother lost her job at the restaurant when her hands and legs became too stiff and enfeebled for her to work. After that, there was never much money. For a while we went on welfare. My mother felt humiliated.

With my father's death Gary's crimes became more desperate, more violent. He talked a friend into helping him commit armed robbery. Gary grabbed the victim's wallet while the friend held a club; he was arrested a short time later, tried and found guilty. The day of his sentencing, during an afternoon when my mother had to work, he called me from the Clackamas County Courthouse. 'How you doing partner? I just wanted to let you and mom know: I got sentenced to fifteen years.'

I was stunned. 'Gary, what can I do for you?' I asked. I think it came out wrong, as if I was saying: I'm busy; what do you *want*?

'I . . . I didn't really want anything,' Gary said, his voice broken. 'I just wanted to hear your voice. I just wanted to say goodbye. You know, I won't be seeing you for a few years. Take care of yourself.' We hadn't shared anything so intimate since that Christmas night, many years before.

My brother Frank had converted to the Jehovah's Witnesses; he'd had enough of both Catholic *and* Mormon theology. In 1966, he was drafted, but refused to learn how to fire a rifle in basic training; his church would not allow its members to carry or use arms in the nation's name. Frank was court-martialed and served three years at Leavenworth Federal Penitentiary. One brother jailed for his tendency to violence; another for his refusal to participate in sanctioned violence.

Gaylen got into progressively worse scrapes. One night, my mother and I were sitting in the kitchen when a car pulled into the driveway and several men piled out. My mother quickly locked the door and dragged me up the stairs into my father's old office. From downstairs, we could hear the men kicking and pounding on the door. 'If you make us come in there to find you, Gilmore, we're going to kill you.' My mother did something I had never known her to do before: she called the police. The pounding and threats continued for several minutes until the sound of a police siren's wail began to make its way up the hill. The men jumped in their car and were gone. A few days later, when Gaylen returned home, my mother told him about the incident. He sat quietly for a while, then asked my mother if she could lend him a hundred dollars; there was something he needed to do. She opened her purse, gave him the money, and Gaylen walked out of the door without saying a word. The next time we heard from him, he was in Salt Lake City, visiting an old friend. He had no plans to return home, he said. Then, a few months later, we heard he was in the hospital, in critical condition. His friend had found him in bed with his wife and stabbed him.

Gaylen recovered and went to Chicago to visit some friends. In 1970 he returned home. He had changed. He was pinched and emaciated. His speech was broken. He still drank too much and was taking pain-killers. He seemed to have lost much of his wit and intelligence. He knocked on my door at two in the morning, in a drunken stupor, and stumbled in and dropped on the sofa, talking incoherently. I put a blanket on him and sat with him until he passed out.

Opposite: Gary Gilmore with his mother, Bessie Gilmore.

Gaylen persuaded his girl-friend from Chicago to join him in Portland. In November 1971, they were married. Two weeks after the wedding, he woke up one night in severe pain; the knife wounds in his stomach and bowel had reopened. He went into the hospital and a few nights later at three in the morning, his wife called me. Gaylen was dead. He was twenty-six years old.

The next morning, my brother Frank and I visited Gary at Oregon State Penitentiary to tell him the news. As he entered the visitors' room, he looked unusually old and tired for a man of thirty. He knew that something was wrong.

'We have bad news for you, Gary,' Frank began.

The warden at Oregon State allowed Gary to attend the funeral. It was the first time the family had gathered together in nine years. It was also the last time.

I didn't have much talent for crime (neither did my brothers, to tell the truth), but I also didn't have much appetite for it. I had seen what my brothers' lives had brought them. For years, my mother had told me that I was the family's last hope for redemption. 'I want *one* son to turn out right, one son I don't have to end up visiting in jail, one son I don't have to watch in court as his life is sentenced away, piece by piece.' After my father's death, she drew me closer to her and her religion, and when I was twelve, I was baptized a Mormon. For many years, the Church's beliefs helped to provide me with a moral centre and a hope for deliverance that I had not known before.

I think culture and history helped to save me. I was born in 1951, and although I remember well the youthful explosion of the 1950s, I was too young to experience it the way my brothers did. The music of Elvis Presley and others had represented and expressed my brothers' rebellion: it was hard-edged, with no apparent ideology. The music was a part of my childhood, but by the early sixties the spirit of the music had been spent.

Then, on 9 February 1964 (my thirteenth birthday, and the day I joined the Mormon priesthood), the Beatles made their first appearance on the Ed Sullivan Show. My life would never be the same. The Beatles meant a change, they promised a world that my parents and brothers could not offer. In fact, I liked the

Beatles in part because they seemed such a departure from the world of my brothers, and because my brothers couldn't abide them.

The rock culture and youth politics of the sixties allowed their adherents to act out a kind of ritualized criminality: we could use drugs, defy authority, or contemplate violent or destructive acts of revolt, we told ourselves, *because we had a reason to.* The music aimed to foment a sense of cultural community, and for somebody who had felt as disenfranchised by his family as I did, rock and roll offered not just a sense of belonging but empowered me with new ideals. I began to find rock's morality preferable to the Mormon ethos, which seemed rigid and severe. One Sunday in the summer of 1967, a member of the local bishopric—a man I admired, and had once regarded as something of a father figure—drove over to our house and asked me to step outside for a talk. He told me that he and other church leaders had grown concerned about my changed appearance—the new length of my hair and my style of dressing—and felt it was an unwelcome influence on other young Mormons. If I did not reject the new youth culture, I would no longer be welcome in church.

On that day a line was drawn. I knew that rock and roll had provided me with a new creed and a sense of courage. I believed I was taking part in a rebellion that mattered—or at least counted for more than my brothers' rebellions. In the music of the Rolling Stones or Doors or Velvet Underground, I could participate in darkness without submitting to it, which is something Gary and Gaylen had been unable to do. I remember their disdain when I tried to explain to them why Bob Dylan was good, why he mattered. It felt great to belong to a different world from them.

And I did: my father and Gaylen were dead; Gary was in prison and Frank was broken. I thought of my family as a cursed outfit, plain and simple, and I believed that the only way to escape its debts and legacies was to leave it. In 1969 I graduated from high school—the only member of my family to do so. The next day, I moved out of the house in Milwaukie and, with some friends, moved into an apartment near Portland State University, in downtown Portland. A short time later, encumbered by overdue property taxes, my mother gave up the nice home on the hill that she had struggled to hold on to. She and my brother Frank bought a small trailer, and settled into a trailer camp.

Gary and I exchanged letters, but whole worlds separated us. In Oregon inmates weren't allowed visitors under the age of eighteen. I felt too guilty to write to Gary about what I was doing in school or about friends and pastimes, because to Gary these existed on the 'outside'. After Gaylen's death, Gary seemed to change. He had lost two members of his family without the opportunity for final reconciliation, and he wanted desperately to be free. In his letters, he began to express more concern for me, more curiosity about what I was doing, who my friends were. He was trying to be my brother. But I told myself I didn't have time for the long trek down to Salem, Oregon, to visit him. I think I was trying to forget him, trying to leave him and our past life behind.

But Gary didn't want to be forgotten.

In the fall of 1972, Gary was granted a 'school release' to attend a community college in Eugene, Oregon, and study art, on the condition that he return to a dorm facility every evening and never leave the Eugene area without the consent of his counsellors. Our family saw it as a turning point.

But on the morning of his release, Gary showed up at my door, a six-pack of beer in his hand. He explained that he wanted to visit friends and family in Portland. 'I'll go back before the night,' he said. 'I can still register tomorrow without getting in any trouble.'

The next afternoon, he showed up again. He was wearing a long black raincoat and a porkpie hat. With his half-grown goatee he looked like a hick hipster. He had a red glare about his eyes. He had not returned to Eugene as he said he would. For his failure to do so he could not only lose his scholarship but be sentenced to additional jail time.

'Gary, what are you doing here?'

He skirted the question. 'Let's get lunch some place. Know

any good places?' I said that there was a restaurant within walking distance, but Gary didn't want to be seen on the streets. He wanted to go by taxi. My anger began to turn to dread. We ended up at a topless bar. As Gary studied the girl on stage, he seemed to be in a trance. I asked him why he wasn't going to school.

He was silent for a long time and stared at the table. When he spoke, it was with his slow, countrified drawl. 'I'm not cut out for school. Man, they can't teach me anything about art that I don't already know. Besides, there are more important things.' He leaned towards me and locked his stare into mine. 'A friend of mine from the joint is being brought up to the dental school here next week. A couple of guards are bringing him up and I want to go see him. Uh, I need a gun. Can you help me?'

I told him he was throwing away his life.

He narrowed his eyes. 'It's a matter of dignity,' he said. Gary stared at me for a long time without expression. He fidgeted with a book of matches. 'I'd do it for *my* brother,' he said.

I saw him only two more times that month. He visited me while I had a girl-friend over and asked me to play Johnny Cash records for him. He was sober and charming. When we were alone, I tried to prod him about his plans. 'Let's just say they've changed,' he said. 'Don't you worry about it. The less you know, the better off you are.'

A few days later I came out of a class at Portland State and Gary was waiting outside. He had borrowed a car and wanted me to meet some friends. We drove out, Gary drinking beer and conversing in a friendly manner. At his friends' house, Gary showed me a collection of his drawings and paintings: drawings of children, studies of ballet dancers and bruised boxers, an occasional depiction of violent death. 'Here,' he said, 'take what you want.' To him, pictures were drawn then given away.

His friends enjoyed luxury that he had never known. While showing me the indoor swimming pool, Gary opened his jacket, took out a pistol and handed it to me, handle first. 'Think you could ever use one of these?' he asked in his best Gary Cooper fashion.

I felt awkward and vulnerable: it was the first time I had ever held a gun. I kept the barrel pointed towards the pool and lifted my finger from the trigger. He took the gun and returned it to his jacket pocket. 'C'mon,' he said. 'I'll drive you home.' We drove back in silence. He seemed angry.

Two nights later I watched a news report of his arrest for armed robbery. My mother and I were unable to visit him in jail, but we attended his trial. Handcuffed and on the verge of tears, Gary acted as his own defence and pleaded for a reprieve. 'I have done a lot of time and I don't think it would do me good to do any more,' he told the judge. 'I have been locked up for the last nine-and-one-half calendar years consecutively, and I have had about two-and-a-half years of freedom since I was fourteen years old. I have always gotten time and have always done it, never been paroled, only had one probation. I have never had a break from the law and I have come to think that justice is kind of harsh and I have never asked for a break until now.'

The judge sentenced Gary to an additional nine years. The next time I saw him was six days before his execution.

In the summer of 1976, I was working at a record store in downtown Portland, making enough money to pay my rent and bills. I was also writing free-lance journalism and criticism, and had sold my first reviews and articles to national publications, including *Rolling Stone*.

On the evening of 30 July, having passed up a chance to go drinking with some friends, I headed home. *The Wild Bunch*, Peckinpah's genuflection to violence and honour, was on television, and as I settled back on the couch to watch it, I picked up the late edition of *The Oregonian*. I almost passed over a page-two item headlined OREGON MAN HELD IN UTAH SLAYINGS, but then something clicked inside me, and I began to read it. 'Gary Mark Gilmore, 35, was charged with the murders of two young clerks during the hold-up of a service station and a motel.' I read on, dazed, about how Gary had been arrested for killing

Opposite: Gary Gilmore at his murder arraignment, July 1976.

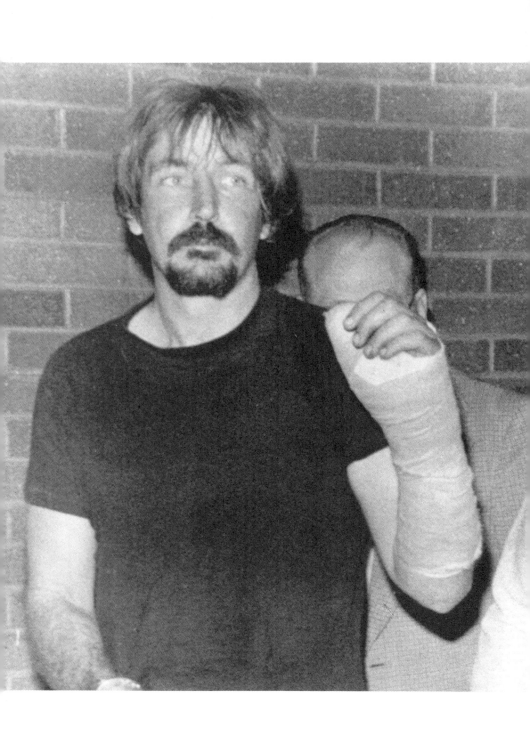

Max Jensen and Ben Bushnell on consecutive nights. Both men were Mormons, about the same age as I, and both left wives and children behind.

I dropped the paper to the floor. I sat on the couch the rest of the night, alternately staring at *The Wild Bunch* and re-reading the sketchy account. I felt shocks of rage, remorse and guilt—as if I were partly responsible for the deaths. I had been part of an uninterested world that had shut Gary away. I had wanted to believe that Gary's life and mine were not entwined, that what had shaped him had not shaped me.

It had been a long time since I had written or visited Gary. After his re-sentencing in 1972, I heard news of him from my mother. In January 1975, Gary was sent to the federal penitentiary in Marion, Illinois. After his transfer, we exchanged a few perfunctory letters. In early April 1976, I learned of the Oregon State Parole Board's decision to parole Gary from Marion to Provo, Utah, rather than transfer him back to Oregon. The transaction had been arranged between the parole board, Brenda Nicol (our cousin) and her father, our uncle Vernon Damico, who lived in Provo. I remember thinking that Gary's being paroled into the heart of one of Utah's most devout and severe Mormon communities was not a great idea.

Between his release and those fateful nights in July, Gary held a job at Uncle Vernon's shoe store, and he met and fell in love with Nicole Barrett, a beautiful young woman with two children. But Gary was unable to deny some old, less wholesome appetites. Almost immediately after his release, he started drinking heavily and taking Fiorinal, a muscle and headache medication that, in sustained doses, can cause severe mood swings and sexual dysfunction. Gary apparently experienced both reactions. He became more violent. Sometimes he got rough with Nicole over failed sex, or over what he saw as her flirtations. He picked fights with other men, hitting them from behind, threatening to cave in their faces with a tyre iron that he twirled as handily as a baton. He lost his job and abused his Utah relatives. He walked into stores and walked out again with whatever he wanted under his arm, glaring at the cashiers, challenging them to try to stop him. He brought guns home, and sitting on the back porch would fire them at trees, fences, the sky. 'Hit the sun,' he told Nicole. 'See if you can make it sink.' Then he hit Nicole with his fist one too many times, and she moved out.

Gary wanted her back. He told a friend that he thought he might kill her.

On a hot night in late July, Gary drove over to Nicole's mother's house and persuaded Nicole's little sister, April, to ride with him in his white pick-up truck. He wanted her to join him in looking for her sister. They drove for hours, listening to the radio, talking aimlessly, until Gary pulled up by a service station in the small town of Orem. He told April to wait in the truck. He walked into the station, where twenty-six-year-old attendant Max Jensen was working alone. There were no other cars there. Gary pulled a .22 automatic from his jacket and told Jensen to empty the cash from his pockets. He took Jensen's coin changer and led the young attendant around the back of the station and forced him to lie down on the bathroom floor. He told Jensen to place his hands under his stomach and press his face to the ground. Jensen complied and offered Gary a smile. Gary pointed the gun at the base of Jensen's skull. 'This one is for me,' Gary said, and he pulled the trigger. And then: 'This one is for Nicole,' and he pulled the trigger again.

The next night, Gary walked into the office of a motel just a few doors away from his uncle Vernon's house in Provo. He ordered the man behind the counter, Ben Bushnell, to lie down on the floor, and then he shot him in the back of the head. He walked out with the motel's cashbox under his arm and tried to stuff the pistol under a bush. But it discharged, blowing a hole in his thumb.

Gary decided to get out of town. First he had to take care of his thumb. He drove to the house of a friend named Craig and telephoned his cousin. A witness had recognized Gary leaving the site of the second murder, and the police had been in touch with Brenda. She had the police on one line, Gary on another. She tried to stall Gary until the police could set up a road-block. After they finished speaking, Gary got into his truck and headed for the local airport. A few miles down the road, he was surrounded by police cars and a SWAT team. He was arrested for Bushnell's murder and confessed to the murder of Max Jensen.

Gary's trial began some months later. The verdict was never in question. Gary didn't help himself when he refused to allow his attorneys to call Nicole as a defence witness. Gary and Nicole had been reconciled; she felt bad for him and visited him in jail every day for hours. Gary also didn't help his case by staring menacingly at the jury members or by offering belligerent testimony on his own behalf. He was found guilty. My mother called me on the night of Gary's sentencing, 7 October, to tell me that he had received the death penalty. He told the judge he would prefer being shot to being hanged.

On 8 November I heard that Gary had waived all rights of appeal and review. He wanted to be executed. Fourth District Judge J. Robert Bullock had complied, setting the date of execution for Monday 15 November. Gary's attorney filed for a stay of execution—against his protests—and the Utah Supreme Court granted one.

I decided to confront Gary about his decision. The next day I called Draper Prison, where he was being held. Our first exchanges were polite and tentative. Gary became impatient. 'Something on your mind?'

I asked if he was serious about requesting execution.

'What do you think?'

'I don't know.'

'That's right. You don't. You never knew me.' Gary had thrown down a barrier I couldn't leap over. I was lost for a reply. 'Look,' he continued, in a softer tone, 'I'm not trying to be mean to you, but this thing's going to happen one way or the other; there's nothing you can do to stop it and I don't particularly want you to like me for it. It'll be easier for me if you don't. It seems the only time we ever talk to each other is around the time of somebody's death. Now it's mine.'

I felt helpless. I asked him to consider mother.

'Well, I want to see mother before all this goes down,' Gary

36

said. 'I want to see all of you. Maybe that will make it easier. But I don't want you or anybody else to interfere. It's my affair. I don't want to spend the rest of my life on trial or in prison. I've lost my freedom. I lost it a long time ago. I don't want you to think I'm some "sensitive" artist because I drew pictures or wrote poems. I killed—in cold blood.' A guard told Gary that his time was up. I asked him to tell his new attorney, Dennis Boaz, to call me. Boaz phoned that night. He said that he supported Gary's right to die and that on the following day, 10 November, he and Gary would appear before the Utah Supreme Court and ask them to lift the stay. I asked Boaz to call me as soon as the court made its decision. He promised to call me by four o'clock the next day. His closing line stayed with me. 'Is it OK if I call you collect? I'm a poor man.'

He didn't call. I learned of his and Gary's successful appearance before the court on the network news, which showed clips of my brother being led from the court-room in shackles, with his wary, piercing stare. Overnight, the most painful and private part of my family's history, a past that I had tried for years to escape, was everywhere. Gary was on the national news nearly every evening of the week; he was on the front page of every newspaper I saw; he was staring out at me from the cover of *Newsweek*. Inside the magazine, I found pictures from my family's photo albums. There was a picture from a distant Christmas with my father, Gary, Gaylen and me, standing in a line. Nobody in the picture looked happy.

Utah governor Calvin Rampton ordered a stay of execution, referring the matter to the state board of pardons and earning the epithet of 'moral coward' from Gary. I received a call on the night of his order from Anthony Amsterdam of Stanford Law School, a well-regarded opponent of the death penalty and a member of the bar of the United States Supreme Court. He outlined a possible course of action for the family: a family member could retain counsel to seek a stay from the US Supreme Court, the duration of which would be determined by the Court's willingness to review the case and the subsequent decision of that review. This meant that Gary would be entitled to a new trial. I passed the information on to mother, who also spoke with

Amsterdam. We agreed to retain him pending the pardons board decision. On Tuesday morning, 16 November, the day after Gary's scheduled execution, Amsterdam called me with the news that Gary and Nicole had attempted suicide with an overdose of sedatives.

On 30 November the pardons board decided to allow the execution to go forward. On 3 December the US Supreme Court granted a stay of execution. Our calls to the prison were turned away. Gary issued an open letter asking my mother to 'butt out'. During this time neither Gary nor his legal representatives attempted to contact any members of the immediate family.

On the morning of 13 December, the Supreme Court lifted its stay, declaring that Gary had made a 'knowing and intelligent waiver of his rights'. The next day Judge Bullock reset the execution for 17 January. Gary was confined to a 'strip cell' and denied visits, even from family members.

By Christmas I told myself and anyone who asked that I didn't care about what might happen. I spent the holidays drunk or drugged. My girl-friend went home to visit her family, and I was with a different woman every night she was gone. I took sleeping pills because I couldn't sleep. When I couldn't sleep, I walked around my house, throwing and breaking things. One night, I dreamed of Gary being tied to a stake and bayoneted repeatedly, while I stood on the other side of a fence, unable to reach him. In the morning, I heard of another, nearly fatal suicide attempt by Gary.

I desperately wanted to see him, to reach out to him at last, to achieve a reconciliation. I was not resigned to his execution.

Draper Prison is located in the Salt Lake Valley at a place known as the 'Point of the Mountain'. The valley is heavily polluted, and one doesn't become aware of the surroundings until the final, winding approach to the prison. Draper rests at the centre of a flat basin, surrounded by tall, sharply inclined snowy slopes. It offers the most beautiful vista in the entire valley.

My brother Frank and I were led into a triangular room in which no guards were present. Gary strolled in. He was dressed in prison whites and in red, white and blue sneakers. He twirled a comb and smiled broadly. I'd seen so many photos and film clips that showed him looking grim and cold that I'd forgotten how charming he could be. 'You're looking as fit as ever,' he said to Frank. 'And you're just as damn skinny as ever,' he said to me. He rearranged the benches in front of the guard room window. 'So those poor fools can keep an eye on me,' he said.

For the first few minutes we exchanged small talk. Then I spoke of the prospect of intervention, but Gary cut me off. 'Look, I don't want anybody interfering, no outside causes, no lawyers like Amsterdam.' He took hold of my chin. 'He's out of this, I hope.' Before I had a chance to reply, the visitors' door opened and Uncle Vernon and Aunt Ida entered. The visit became an ordeal. Gary and Vernon did most of the talking, discussing the people Gary wanted to leave money to and cracking macabre jokes. Vernon had brought along a bag of green T-shirts adorned with a computerized photo of Gary and the legend, 'Gilmore—death wish'. Vernon and Gary discussed the possibility of Gary wearing one on the morning of the execution and Vernon auctioning it off to the highest bidder.

As we were leaving, Gary offered me a T-shirt. I didn't accept it.

'Well,' he drawled, smiling, 'it's a little big for you, but I think you can grow into it.' I took the shirt.

I visited Gary again. I forced myself to ask the question I'd been building up to: 'What would you do if we were able to stop this?'

'I don't want you to do that,' he said gravely.

'That doesn't answer my question.'

'I'd kill myself. Look, I'm not watched closely in this place. I could've killed myself any time in the last two weeks. But I don't want to. Besides, if a person's dumb enough to murder and get caught, then he shouldn't snivel about what he gets.'

Gary went on to talk about prison life, describing some of the brutality he had witnessed and some that he had fostered. He was terrified of a life in prison. 'Maybe you could have my sentence commuted, but you wouldn't have to live that sentence or be around when I killed myself.' The fear in his eyes was most discernible when he spoke about prison, far more than when he spoke about his own impending death—maybe because one was an abstraction and the other an ever-present concrete reality. 'I don't think death will be anything new or frightening for me. I think I've been there before.'

We talked for hours, or rather Gary talked. This was the first real communication we had had in years; neither of us wanted to let go. I told Gary that I was supposed to leave that night, to go back home and spend the weekend with mother. 'Can't you stay for one more day?' he asked. I agreed to return the next day.

I reached our lawyer and told him that I had decided not to intervene to block the execution. Telling him was almost as hard as making the decision. I could have sought a stay, signed the necessary documents and gone away feeling that I had made the right decision, the moral choice. But I didn't have to bear the weight of that decision; Gary did. If I could have chosen for Gary to live, I would have.

On Saturday 15 January, I saw Gary for the last time. Camera crews were camped in the town of Draper, preparing for the finale.

During our other meetings that week, Gary had opened with friendly remarks or a joke or even a handstand. This day, though, he was nervous and was eager to deny it. We were separated by a glass partition. 'Naw, the noise in this place gets to me sometimes, but I'm as cool as a cucumber,' he said, holding up a steady hand. The muscles in his wrists and arms were taut and thick as rope.

Gary showed me letters and pictures he'd received, mainly from children and teenage girls. He said he always tried to answer the ones from kids first, and he read one from an eight-year-old boy: 'I hope they put you some place and make you live forever for what you did. You have no right to die. With all the malice in my heart. [*name*.]'

'Man, that one shook me up for a long time,' he said.

I asked him if he'd replied to it.

'Yeah, I wrote, "You're too young to have malice in your

heart. I had it in mine at a young age and look what it did for me.'"

Gary's eyes nervously scanned some letters and pictures, finally falling on one that made him smile. He held it up. A picture of Nicole. 'She's pretty, isn't she?' I agreed. 'I look at this picture every day. I took it myself; I made a drawing from it. Would you like to have it?'

I said I would. I asked him where he would have gone if he had made it to the airport the night of the second murder.

'Portland.'

I asked him why.

Gary studied the shelf in front of him. 'I don't want to talk about that night any more,' he said. 'There's no *point* in talking about it.'

'Would you have come to see me?'

He nodded. For a moment his eyes flashed the old anger. 'And what would *you* have done if I'd come to you?' he asked. 'If I had come and said I was in trouble and needed help, needed a place to stay? Would *you* have taken me in? Would you have hidden me?'

The question had been turned back on me. I couldn't speak. Gary sat for a long moment, holding me with his eyes, then said steadily: 'I think I was coming to kill you. I think that's what would have happened; there may have been no choice for you, no choice for me.' His eyes softened. 'Do you understand why?'

I nodded. Of course I understood why: I had escaped the family—or at least thought I had. Gary had not.

I felt terror. Gary's story could have been mine. Then terror became relief—Jensen and Bushnell's deaths, and Gary's own impending death, had meant my own safety. I finished the thought, and my relief was shot through with guilt and remorse. I felt closer to Gary than I'd ever felt before. I understood why he wanted to die.

The warden entered Gary's room. They discussed whether Gary should wear a hood for the execution.

I rapped on the glass partition and asked the warden if he would allow us a final handshake. At first he refused but consented after Gary explained it was our final visit, on the condition that I agree to a skin search. After I had been searched by two guards, two other guards brought Gary around the partition. They said that I would have to roll up my sleeve past my elbow, and that we could not touch beyond a handshake. Gary grasped my hand, squeezed it tight and said, 'Well, I guess this is it.' He leaned over and kissed me on the cheek.

On Monday morning, 17 January, in a cannery warehouse out behind Utah State Prison, Gary met his firing-squad. I was with my mother and brother and girl-friend when it happened. Just moments before, we had seen the morning newspaper with the headline EXECUTION STAYED. We switched on the television for more news. We saw a press conference. Gary's death was being announced.

There was no way to be prepared for that last see-saw of emotion. You force yourself to live through the hell of knowing that somebody you love is going to die in an expected way, at a specific time and place, and that there is nothing you can do to change that. For the rest of your life, you will have to move around in a world that wanted this death to happen. You will have to walk past people every day who were heartened by the killing of somebody in your family—somebody who you knew had long before been murdered emotionally.

You turn on the television, and the journalist tells you how the warden put a black hood over Gary's head and pinned a small, circular cloth target above his chest, and how five men pumped a volley of bullets into him. He tells you how the blood flowed from Gary's devastated heart and down his chest, down his legs, staining his white pants scarlet and dripping to the warehouse floor. He tells you how Gary's arm rose slowly at the moment of the impact, how his fingers seemed to wave as his life left him.

Shortly after Gary's execution, *Rolling Stone* offered me a job as an assistant editor at their Los Angeles bureau. It was a nice offer. It gave me the chance to get away from Portland and all the bad memories it represented.

I moved to Los Angeles in April 1977. It was not an easy life at first. I drank a pint of whisky every night, and I took Dalmane, a sleeping medication that interfered with my ability to dream—or at least made it hard to remember my dreams. There were other lapses: I was living with one woman and seeing a couple of others. For a season or two my writing went to hell. I didn't know what to say or how to say it; I could no longer tell if I had anything *worth* writing about. I wasn't sure how you made words add up. Instead of writing, I preferred reading. I favoured hard-boiled crime fiction—particularly the novels of Ross Macdonald—in which the author tried to solve murders by explicating labyrinthine family histories. I spent many nights listening to punk rock. I liked the music's accommodation with a merciless world. One of the most famous punk songs of the period was by the Adverts. It was called 'Gary Gilmore's Eyes.' What would it be like, the song asked, to see the world through Gary Gilmore's dead eyes? Would you see a world of murder?

All around me I had Gary's notoriety to contend with. During my first few months in LA—and throughout the years that followed—most people asked me about my brother. They wanted to know what Gary was like. They admired his bravado, his hardness. I met a woman who wanted to sleep with me because I was his brother. I tried to avoid these people.

I also met women who, when they learned who my brother was, would not see me again, not take my calls again. I received letters from people who said I should not be allowed to write for a young audience. I received letters from people who thought I should have been shot alongside my brother.

There was never a time without a reminder of the past. In 1979, Norman Mailer's *The Executioner's Song* was published. At the time, I was living with a woman I loved very much. As she read the book, I could see her begin to wonder about who she was sleeping with, about what had come into her life. One night, a couple of months after the book had been published, we were watching *Saturday Night Live*. The guest host was doing a routine of impersonations. He tied a bandana around his eyes and gleefuly announced his next subject: 'Gary Gilmore!' My girl-friend got up from the sofa and moved into the bedroom, shutting the door. I poured a glass of whisky. She came out a few

43

minutes later. 'I'm sorry,' she said, 'I can't live with you any more. I can't stand being close to all this stuff.' She was gone within a week.

I watched as a private and troubling event continued to be the subject of public sensation and media scrutiny; I watched my brother's life—and in some way, my life—become too large to control. I tried not to surrender to my feelings because my feelings wouldn't erase the pain or shame or bad memories or unresolved love and hate. I was waiting to be told what to feel.

I tried to leave the reality of my family behind me. I visited my mother in Oregon a couple of times a year, but the visits were always disturbing. She talked incessantly about the past—about her childhood in Utah, about Gary's death, about the family curse—and her health was bad. After Gary's death, she refused to leave her trailer, and my brother Frank and I could not convince her to see a doctor.

In the last few years of her life, my mother began to tell my brother Frank and me stories that were like confessions. She told us how she had hated her father: he had been a cruel and authoritarian Mormon patriarch; he had beaten his children with a whip; he had tormented and humiliated her brother George terribly. She never forgave him for dragging her to the hanging in the meadow. She had not, in fact, managed to keep her face buried in his side that morning. In the instant before the trapdoor was pulled, her father grabbed her by the hair and yanked hard, forcing her to watch the man as he dropped to death. On the ride back, she decided that she would never forgive her father, and that she would live a life to spite his hard virtue.

In June 1980, her stomach ruptured. She was sitting in the small front room of her trailer, talking to my brother about all the pain her father and her husband had left her with, and she started to lose blood. We brought her to the hospital. She fell into a coma, and a few days later she died.

I helped my brother bury her. Frank was forty years old,

Opposite: Gary Gilmore arrives in court to hear the judge set the third date for his execution, 15 December 1975.

and he seemed lost without her.

The night of her funeral, Frank and I stayed at a friend's house. I had to fly back to Los Angeles the next day. I told Frank to come to California and stay with me for a while. In the morning we said goodbye. I watched him turn and walk away. I wrote to him as soon as I got back to LA. Within a few days, the letter came back. It was marked: NO LONGER AT THIS ADDRESS. NO FORWARDING ADDRESS. For a long time I tried to find him, but I never did. I have not seen him since that morning we said goodbye to each other on that haunted stretch of Oregon highway. He seemed to have walked into the void with all the other ghosts.

A few months after my mother's death, I fell in love. Like me, she came from a family with a history of death and brutality. We believed we could help each other make up for our losses and in August 1982 we were married.

The marriage did not last—how could it? My wife and I brought along too many family demons for one house. I hadn't so much loved her as tried to save her, in order to atone for my failure to save my brother. I went on to pursue one vain relationship after another, in a desperate attempt to discover or build the sort of family that had not been present in my childhood. I sometimes sabotaged these relationships, as a way of never having the family life I claimed I wanted so much—of *not* passing to my children the inheritance of violence and ruin that I feared might be genetic. For far too long, I stopped wanting any home or family, because it hurt too much, felt too much like irredeemable failure, to want those things and yet feel I would never have them, or might damage them once I did have them.

And then, a few years ago, I decided I was ready to move back home. I believed I could live again in the place where so much ruin had occurred and simply ignore all that ruin; I thought I might seize those dreams I had wanted for so long. But I came face-to-face with that damn family spectre, and it devastated my life and also my hope, and I returned to my friends and life in Los Angeles.

Can murder's momentum end? It has been fifty years since Gary was born. It has been over fourteen years since he committed his murders and died for them. You would think that would be enough time to forget, to redeem. But the past never stops.

Early one evening a few months ago a friend called to tell me that *A Current Affair*—a nationally syndicated programme that takes real-life scandal and repackages it into a news-entertainment format—would be running a segment that night on my brother. The show's producers had tracked down Nicole and persuaded her to grant an interview about Gary and his murders and execution—the first lengthy television interview she had ever agreed to do.

It came as a bit of a surprise to me that, after well over a decade, Gary's relationship with Nicole and his death would still be hot news. Maybe it was a slow day for scandalmongering. I tuned in the programme, expecting something tasteless, and what I saw was certainly that. But it was also strangely affecting in ways I had not expected: there was news footage of Gary being led to and from court during the many hearings of those last few months, handcuffed and dressed in prison whites, his wary, appraising eyes scanning the cameras that surrounded and documented him. I remembered watching this footage back in the daze and fury of 1976. Fourteen years later he looked cold-blooded, arrogant, deadly. He also looked plain scared, and he looked like *my* brother. That is, like somebody I both loved and hated; somebody who had transformed my life in ways that could never be repaired; somebody I had missed very much in the years since his death and I wished I could talk with, no matter how painful the talking might be.

The programme's message was sordid and mean-spirited. The point, it seemed, was to try to hang much of the blame for Gary's murders on Nicole. Nicole described the last time Gary had hit her. 'I had been hit before by men,' she said, 'and I told myself, "I'm leaving." No matter what I did, I did not deserve that. He knew that was how I felt. And when I looked at him, I knew that when I went, he would kill someone. I knew that if I left him, somebody would die for it.'

'And yet you left anyway?' the interviewer asked.

Nicole looked off camera for a moment. 'One of the greater regrets of my life,' she said.

The interviewer's implication couldn't have been plainer: Nicole shared in the blame. 'How could you say you loved somebody so cold-blooded?' he asked at the end.

'There isn't a day goes by,' said Nicole, 'his name doesn't go through my head. He came into my life, he loved me, and he destroyed all the good that was there.'

'If you could erase Gary Gilmore from your life, would you?'

Again, another glance away, and she shook her head.

'And you say that,' the interviewer asked, 'knowing that if you erased Gary those two men would still be alive, those men's children would still have their fathers . . . '

Finally, Nicole closed off the question. 'Yeah,' she said, nodding. 'Yeah, then I would.'

The camera cut to the programme's host, who had an expression of smug disgust. 'Tough to shed a tear for her,' he said.

I turned off the television and the lights in my front room, and I sat in the dark for hours.

Only a few months before, I had gone through one of the worst times of my life—my brief move to Portland and back. What had gone wrong, I realized, was because of my past, something that had been set in motion long before I was born. It was what Gary and I shared, more than any blood tie: we were both heirs to a legacy of negation that was beyond our control or our understanding. Gary had ended up turning the nullification outward—on innocents, on Nicole, on his family, on the world and its ideas of justice, finally on himself. I had turned the ruin inward. Outward or inward—either way, it was a powerfully destructive legacy, and for the first time in my life, I came to see that it had not really finished its enactment. To believe that Gary had absorbed all the family's dissolution, or that the worst of that rot had died with him that morning in Draper, Utah, was to

Opposite: Journalists examine the chair to which Gary Gilmore was strapped for execution.

miss the real nature of the legacy that had placed him before those rifles: what that heritage or patrimony was about, and where it had come from.

We tend to view murders as solitary ruptures in the world around us, outrages that need to be attributed and then punished. There is a motivation, a crime, an arrest, a trial, a verdict and a punishment. Sometimes—though rarely—that punishment is death. The next day, there is another murder. The next day, there is another. There has been no punishment that breaks the pattern, that stops this custom of one murder following another.

Murder has worked its way into our consciousness and our culture in the same way that murder exists in our literature and film: we consume each killing until there is another, more immediate or gripping one to take its place. When *this* murder story is finished, there will be another to intrigue and terrify that part of the world that has survived it. And then there will be another. Each will be a story; each will be treated and reported and remembered as a unique incident. Each murder will be solved, but murder itself will never be solved. You cannot solve murder without solving the human heart or the history that has rendered that heart so dark and desolate.

This murder story is told from inside the house where murder was born. It is the house where I grew up, and it is a house that I have never been able to leave.

As the night passed, I formed an understanding of what I needed to do. I would go back into my family—into its stories, its myths, its memories, its inheritance—and find the real story and hidden propellants behind it. I wanted to climb into the family story in the same way I've always wanted to climb into a dream about the house where we all grew up.

In the dream, it is always night. We are in my father's house—a charred-brown, 1950s-era home. Shingled, two-storey and weather-worn, it is located on the far outskirts of a dead-end American town, pinioned between the night-lights and smoking chimneys of towering industrial factories. A moonlit stretch of railroad track forms the border to a forest I am forbidden to trespass. A train whistle howls in the distance. No train ever comes.

People move from the darkness outside the house to the darkness inside. They are my family. They are all back from the dead. There is my mother, Bessie Gilmore, who, after a life of bitter losses, died spitting blood, calling the names of her father and her husband—men who had long before brutalized her hopes and her love—crying to them for mercy, for a passage into the darkness that she had so long feared. There is my brother Gaylen, who died young of knife-wounds, as his new bride sat holding his hand, watching the life pass from his sunken face. There is my brother Gary, who murdered innocent men in rage against the way life had robbed him of time and love, and who died when a volley of bullets tore his heart from his chest. There is my brother Frank, who became quieter and more distant with each new death, and who was last seen in the dream walking down a road, his hands rammed deep into his pockets, a look of uncomprehending pain on his face. There is my father, Frank Sr, dead of the ravages of lung cancer. He is in the dream less often than the other family members, and I am the only one happy to see him.

One night, years into the same dream, Gary tells me why I can never join my family in its comings and goings, why I am left alone sitting in the living-room as they leave: it is because I have not yet entered death. I cannot follow them across the tracks, into the forest where their real lives take place, until I die. He pulls a gun from his coat pocket. He lays it on my lap. There is a door across the room, and he moves towards it. Through the door is the night. I see the glimmer of the train tracks. Beyond them, my family.

I do not hesitate. I pick the pistol up. I put its barrel in my mouth. I pull the trigger. I feel the back of my head erupt. It is a softer feeling than I expected. I feel my teeth fracture, disintegrate and pass in a gush of blood out of my mouth. I feel my life pass out of my mouth, and in that instant, I collapse into nothingness. There is darkness, but there is no beyond. There is *never* any beyond, only the sudden, certain rush of extinction. I know that it is death I am feeling—that is, I know this is how death must truly feel and I know that this is where beyond ceases to be a possibility.

I have had the dream more than once, in various forms. I always wake up with my heart hammering hard, hurting after being torn from the void that I know is the gateway to the refuge of my ruined family. Or is it the gateway to hell? Either way, I want to return to the dream, but in the haunted hours of the night there is no way back.

MODERN PAINTERS

★

AMERICAN ISSUE

OUT

NOW!

★

'No other magazine has played
such an influential role
and none since the war has
stimulated such debate.'
Nicholas Serota

★

'The best art magazine
of our time.'
Paul Johnson

Telephone:
081-995 1909

Fax:
081-742 1462

Address
**10 Barley Mow Passage
London W4 4PH**

ART, BODIES AND DE SADE

Art, Mimesis and the Avant-Garde
Aspects of a Philosophy of Difference
Andrew Benjamin, University of Warwick
An exploration of the relationship between art and philosophy that leads Andrew Benjamin to original reinterpretations of contemporary painters including Lucien Freud, Francis Bacon and R.B. Kitaj.
August 1991: 320pp: 216x138: illus.
7 b+w photographs
Hb: 0-415-06047-8: £40.00
Pb: 0-415-06627-1: £12.99

Fabrications
Costume and the Female Body
Edited by **Charlotte Herzog**, William Rainey Harper College, and
Jane Gaines, Duke University
A fascinating collection of essays that examines the changing representation of the female body in film from the 1950s Sweetheart fashion to the contemporary female body builder.
AFI Film Readers
July 1991: 304pp: 229x152: illus.
Hb: 0-415-90061-1: £30.00
Pb: 0-415-90062-X: £8.99

New in Paperback
From Sappho to De Sade
Moments in the History of Sexuality
Edited by **Jan Bremmer**, University of Groningen
Contributors explore various aspects of sexuality in successive periods such as heterosexuality, lesbianism and incest, which remain at the centre of modern debates and reflect its tangled history.
May 1991: 224pp: 216x138: illus. 16 b+w photographs
Pb: 0-415-06300-0: £10.99

Manful Assertions
Masculinities in Britain Since 1800
Edited by **Michael Roper**, London Business School and **John Tosh**, Polytechnic of North London
A collection of essays that merges current discussions in sexual politics with historical analysis that shows that masculinity is not a natural monolithic concept but an ever changing cultural construct.
July 1991: 240pp: 216x138: illus.
Hb: 0-415-05322-6: £30.00
Pb: 0-415-05323-4: £9.99

ROUTLEDGE

Available through booksellers. In case of difficulty, or for more information contact: James Powell, Routledge, 11 New Fetter Lane, London EC4P 4EE. Tel: 071 - 583 9855

SAPPHO DURRELL
JOURNALS AND LETTERS

Lawrence Durrell, Claude Durrell and Sappho Durrell, 1961.

On 21 September 1984, Sappho Durrell, the second daughter of the novelist Lawrence Durrell, visited her neighbour and friend Barbara Robson. She wanted Barbara Robson's help in preparing a will and asked if she would act as her executrix. She also asked her to accept several carrier-bags of her writings. These included journals, a play about Emily Brontë, dream notebooks and correspondence, mainly between Sappho Durrell and her father. The writings, according to Barbara Robson, were to be kept away from the family, and she was to use her best efforts to see that they were published after the deaths of both Sappho Durrell and her father. Four months later, on 31 January 1985, Sappho Durrell committed suicide. Five years later Lawrence Durrell died.

Lawrence Durrell was married four times, and Sappho, born in 1951 in Oxford, was a daughter of the second marriage. After the birth the family eventually returned to Cyprus, where the mother, Eve Cohen, had a nervous breakdown and asked Lawrence Durrell's mother to move in to look after Sappho. Two years later Eve and Lawrence Durrell separated. Sappho Durrell moved to England with her mother but continued to visit her father regularly and developed a close relationship with his new wife, Claude, especially after they settled in France. In 1967, Claude unexpectedly died of cancer. Sappho was sixteen.

Durrell's novels are, like many authors', autobiographically informed, and parallels can be found between his own life and the characters in his fiction. Sappho believed that she was the inspiration for at least one of Durrell's characters, Livia, from the novel of the same name published in 1978. Livia is a changeling, a monster created by a bad sperm that passed between an occidental and an oriental (Sappho's mother Eve was an Alexandrian Jew), who grew up to be an androgyne and Sapphist. She is said to have been a girl forged from a boy, who dreamed she had sex for the first time with a man who resembled her father and later became a lesbian. Livia dies by suicide: she hangs herself.

This edited selection from the journals and letters is drawn mainly from 1979, the year Sappho Durrell underwent psychoanalysis under the care of Patrick Casement.

I want to play around with the idea of parricide—not in general but in specific. Vis à vis my father.

We went to visit the tomb and found dogroses and Venus' mirror on Claude's grave. On the way back, in the strange light, he began to improvise a Poe-like story very badly to demonstrate how the Languedoc lent itself to this, but more generally to show how the world was inside, waiting for its spring to be tapped, for the story-teller to tap it. I understood all this, tacitly, rationally, but in me I felt so dead: like a gourd with a good shape, but dry. I know that, *rationally*, he would like me to stand up and create, but that there is something in him which would 'kill' me if I did—would knock what I did. I will always have his ego between me and the world, and my surroundings will be as dry as dust.

Suddenly I try to imagine travelling this same road, with the castle and the trees, and supposing him dead. At once the colours around me deepen. In my mind I begin to breathe deeply, and my heart seems to beat faster. The world becomes infinite and excites me with its possibilities. My father dead, and perhaps killed by me?

I seem to suffer from the hypochondriac obsession that I will die early and that he wants me to die before him.

Some fortuitous things happened today. That film which had such an effect on me—probably quite out of proportion with its true merit—*A Bigger Splash*. The pool in the final picture haunted me. Hockney in the film referred to the fact that it was half painted in Albert's Hyde Park and half painted by a pool lent by a friend in the south of France. It struck me, when I saw Armand's pool, that it could have been there—in the mountains. There can't be many places that have mountains covered in woods, with these same proportions.

Florence took me to her house—very California—and from the balcony we looked down the mountainside past the two or three turquoise patches of swimming pools to one at the very bottom—a paler turquoise, with a man, a good three kilometres away, drying himself in a huge corn-coloured towel. Florence said—'*Tiens, ça appartient à un peintre anglais, qui paraît au tournage d'un film très populaire en Angleterre, au bord de cette piscine.'* It was in fact David Hockney who she was referring to—coincidence.

It was like looking down on a myth—this tiny slip of blue three kilometres down—was the very scene which held so much imaginative meaning for me. *Le point du départ quoi.* The pool belongs to Tony Richardson, and I can visit them tomorrow: to pay my pilgrimage. Something that Peter Adams had said earlier in the day came back to me like a perfume: 'Nothing is real outside the head; all is illusory except what is in the mind.' When one's world is polluted to the soles of the shoes—then the mind must recreate a liveable world. Hockney for me was one of those starting points for imagining a world one can taste again.

22 MARCH 1979: Somewhere in the Po Valley there is a gap in the wall that runs alongside the main highway. The gap leads to a minor road which turns finally into a cart-track. This is the way to Mudu's house. Once there the Po Valley suddenly falls into place, and the journey makes sense, but until then it had the aura of a dream. It was all arbitrary and unknown.

Mudu is a hermaphrodite. This is never said of course; only suggested. Mudu (Modo, Prince of Darkness) belongs to that category of country lesbians, the friends of friends' parents whom I met when I was at school: pert, shrewd, fixing you with an eye that has all the sharpness and flatness of a cod. That same ancient sour cynicism.

Well, come in, Mudu said. It's all in order! I heard that you needed a rest—one without influence; I think that was the term you used, and here there has never been influence of any kind. Consider this your personal retreat.

I was in no position to take him at other than his word. I was recovering from a bad psychological set-back and I'd given up bothering my mind with questions about others' motives. I had resolved on short, sharp tactics if things developed unpleasantly or became too demanding (as they had in all my other relationships).

I arrived in the early evening. It was rather like going into a retreat—shriven, gentle. Mudu insisted that I have a bath ('To wash away that filthy train grime') and began preparing the meal only when I emerged from the bathroom. Throughout my stay, there were gentle rituals and I had long periods on my own. There was something monastic about Mudu—even his use of talk, wine, food and objects—and I soon found that my tempo eased and I began to savour my surroundings more. I had the slight and not unpleasant feeling that I was waiting for something.

I didn't notice anything unusual for a while: there are so many strange new things about foreign parts generally and Italy particularly that I was lost for whole mornings wandering in the garden, smelling the new smells, comparing fauna and trying to define differences in atmosphere. It took me some time to focus on Mudu again and notice that his character was not a product of sun and wine, and that his profound distrust and disgust with the world was more than a reactionary trooper's reflexes. Although he had a veneer of the old guard, with its right-wing opinions on a host of worldly matters, he had little practical experience of the world. His manner to me was not the one I had learned to expect from a middle-aged man to a young woman. He never patronized me in the slightest.

5 APRIL 1979: Dr Casement. First appointment.

7 APRIL 1979: Second session. In my dream I made love to my mother. I remembered it when I got back from seeing Casement, and, though I hadn't been upset when dreaming, I now cried on remembering it. I was making love to her, even though I was disgusted, and I was having to force her—she was being coy and forcing me away. I wanted to make love to her not out of desire but out of domination. I hated her, despised her, and yet I went on. It was much how I imagine a man feels.

The moment you didn't respond to my attempts to charm you I immediately imagined you were:

One. Bored, tired.

Two. Angry and unable to cope with me and my problems; not wanting to.

Three. Hostile. Censorious, disapproving.

Four. Malevolent.

10 APRIL 1979: Analysis has never worked.

The first analyst—I had a peculiarly upsetting run of dreams. Shook me. I dried up. My memory blanked out. He asked me for associations but I couldn't think of any. He gave up after a while. Session over. He told my mother that I had burst into tears—which was not true—and that he thought I was a schizophrenic.

The problem is centred around expression. It's all tied up, so much so that I need constant prompting by an analyst. My mind doesn't want to let anything out, but I do. It's programmed to cut at certain intervals. I feel very precarious.

30 APRIL 1979: CASEMENT'S INVOICE. Six sessions in April: £64.

1 MAY 1979: Trying to think why my relationship with my father is now so fucked up. I used to write him letters, but since Claude died his traditional pattern of *wife=whore/stupid/bitch* and *me= virgin/wise* has disintegrated. Because none of the women he has had since Claude died ever measured up to her, he has been placing more and more of the wife's role on me and he is *always* aggressive towards wives. They can't do anything right except be sweet and kind and giving. Before, when I withdrew, he would accept that I was different. Now he is aggressive, using the psychology of hostile silences or bitchiness. He is a master in the art of psychological destruction. He knows just where to hit.

I feel, when I'm with him—or writing to him—that I am on his black side. We quarrel over a shirt label; he will not give in over a single detail of reality. I am frightened of him physically and mentally.

2 MAY 1979: I'd better start at the beginning.

Father. Born 1912. India. His father: an engineer for the railways who died suddenly of heart attack when his son was twelve; he remembers his father as very tall. When born, Lawrence was jaundiced and appeared to be dead. It was only when they had administered to his mother and she was found to be OK that they looked in the basket and noticed that he was alive. His mother: hatred/love. She and he were very close. A sick baby. Once he mentioned that he had read a biography of

Florence Nightingale and that it had helped him to understand her psychology. It could be that the relationship between them was nurse/patient—much like Proust—and his hold could never be physical but mental and psychological. BUT: he *is* very tough physically. He is wiry with a liver like a punch bag: he's pummelled it so much with drink that it's a rock.

Father's marriages: there were four.

The first: Nancy, a painter. They had a daughter Penelope (Pinky), but Nancy found him overpowering. She had an affair, but he said that it was OK and that she could burn the affair out of her system and return to him when she felt like it. She hit roof. She wanted him to be possessive (wanted, really, to get away from him unbeknown to herself?). She said that he was a monster and that she would leave and take the child. She did. My Dad never fought for her. He just washed his hands and said let's see what Nancy can make of her. Pinky was two at the time, and he did not see her again until she was fifteen or seventeen.

Pinky is very, very repressed and unreal. She is petrified of emotions which are too strong—anything other than twee.

Marriage two. My mother. Eve.

My mother had a bitch of an unloving mother and a father who was obviously sexually attracted to her (never consummated, my mother says—which is true). When my mother met my father she was in the process of having a mini-breakdown and she just talked and talked to shed everything. He listened very understandingly at the time but was later able to use the things that came out against her. My father, an aggressive and demonic drunkard, has always lived on the edge of madness, and at the end of his tipsy stages he becomes very destructive, with a terrible psychological accuracy. It doesn't matter who it is. I remember I never thought him violent until he hit me. They lived together from 1942 to 1947 and were married in 1947.

I was born in 1951. On the day of 28 May, the hospital saw that the birth was going to be in the middle of the night, so they drugged my mother to set back the contractions. My mother didn't want to be drugged. She fought as much as she could. And I was born two days later, with my head all scrunched up and my eyes like slits—at two in the morning. My father's first comment was that my mother must have been having an affair with a Korean.

My father apparently was enchanted with me. So was Mother, but after eighteen months their relationship started to go sour, and my mother began to get very depressed. She tried to explain to my father how depressed she felt by saying, 'It was like you felt in Argentina,' (he nearly cracked-up, collapsed with acute depression there; my mother had to nurse him), but he pooh-poohed her. No one could suffer as much as a great artist.

She didn't know how to make him understand how serious her illness was. She had become frightened of his violence and had decided to leave. She was talking to herself in bed, saying that she would tell him tomorrow, and a voice in her head said, 'You *won't*,' and, suddenly, the bedroom blind accidentally shot up with a bang, waking my father. He asked her what she had done.

My mother said, 'It wasn't me—but since you're awake, I'm leaving you.'

He said, 'Is that all? Let's discuss this in the morning.'

My mother said, 'No. Now.'

He got up and they started arguing. They went into the hall and she went on screaming, 'I'm leaving I'm leaving.' He started to argue but when he saw that her ring was gone, the breath went out of him. He wheezed with the shock and started to throw her around. Instead of fighting back as she usually did, she submitted because he couldn't hurt her. Three days three nights they played cat and mouse. He became the devil. He refused to believe she had the will to leave him. She peed on the bed. It was a pure power struggle. At the end of the three days he was frightened of her. She was frightened herself. She was having hallucinations.

Amid all this, I needed to have my nappies changed, which my mum did but, as she was changing them, she looked up and saw in my father's face an awful demonic look. It was as plain as day. As soon as he realized that she had seen it, he caught himself and re-composed his features.

She was drugged and taken to a military hospital. They drugged her heavily to the point where her head was throbbing.

While my mother was away, I was looked after by my

grandmother but she disliked having to deal with my shitting (servants had dealt with it in India with her children). My father echoed her disgust and disapproval. She said that when my mother came back she was going to punish me for shitting in my pants (I still had to wear corduroy trousers to keep nappies up). On her return my mother was horrified to see my fright.

When she finally came back she was fully recovered and wanted to take me away (she remembered the devil). It became a battle for my soul—who was closest to me.

Hair washing finally blew the gasket. I had got soap in my eye once and screamed like hell if anyone mentioned hair washing. In the end my hair was matted it was so dirty. My mother decided a hairdresser was the only way. 'Here, *take* your daughter,' my granny said, and thrust me against my mother.

Confrontation came when they said that my mother should leave but that I was to stay. It happened in the hall, apparently. They both marched up with me between them, holding each of their hands, and said that my mother was to get out: she was upsetting me; she was being a spanner in the works. I dropped their hands and went to my mother.

Points to raise with Casement: One. 'You're hurting me.' It's from my mother, but I can't remember anyone having hurt her (me? my father?). The phrase sticks in my mind. Also the tone of voice she used. Whining, ingratiating, half surprised, half manipulative.

Two. Imagined conversation with analyst: that it was worse than going to the dentist. It was in a sense a mental violation. It was unclean, disgusting, unfair—obscene. Probing the mind.

3 MAY 1979: Media—used not to be a factor in our relationship but has become more so. Perhaps father feels that as his life becomes more empty he needs to fill it with unimportant chatter.

DIALOGUE: She, fingering glass: really just a buck for my wit to jump over. The late sixties were the catchment area of the cynic. Now people seem to be settling again on the sentimental.

He: You mean you'd settle for the sentimental.

She: Well, *no*. My sense of the times—say, gauged by songs, like, for instance, 'Who wants yesterday's papers?'—is completely dated now. Everyone is dying for yesterday's *anything*. People are either honestly ostrich-like, or at least, as they'd put it, more mellow in their disenchantment . . . [*Looks at her watch*] and at 23.37 hours you can quote me on that—

He: Come over here. [*Winning.*] You can bring your glass if you're afraid of coming alone.

Silence.

She: I don't like to be made to feel so little-womanish.

He: I'm not interested in you as a woman. Right at this moment. I can feel my blood withdrawing from my skin and shrinking into my centres, and a little bit of warm companionship helps. Am I such a conger eel as all that? Come on, unlace a bit. [*He pats cushion once. She sits.*] I hate being lectured at. Let's talk about you.

[*She is watching darkly and looks suspicious, but is actually stiff and awkward.*]

She: I'm level. As the situation stands or falls, I see I have no choice. No. Let's talk about *you*.

The Barrier Reef. While lying asleep in a northern snow and with a mute ear plug in one ear, I heard a lazy, fat, noisy fly (there were no flies originally—I caught them all in glasses and set them out in my first two days here . . .) circling heavily around the room. Limbs, stagnant, floating came with me into view.

In memory, fourteen years ago—for a second the room was dazed with sun—an afternoon siesta in southern France.

Siestas always depressed me. Stagnant, buzzing flesh. The endless wail of crickets on the wits, and Mr Bowlbelly and his welts of flesh and the seams of spit shining in sulky lines from his open mouth.

A point—when I could no longer use my own distress creatively—to grow. Something seemed to have snapped, that might have caused other dislocations ever since.

Only your hair is trembling: as I watch it I am milked moment by moment of definition.

Prometheus

He laid his starchy finger on my brain
And told me I must bleed
To have my orgasms picked out of my body
To have on his lip 'fall and cease'.
And my limbs lay about me like mustard on a bone.
Something rich shit enjoys.

His balls lay in the crook of his lap—
As if he were offering them disgusted:
'Here take this and bury it somewhere
for me.'

I worry about the idea that the men's movement should work for warm, loving relationships between men. I see no evidence that men have ever had much difficulty in relating to each other intellectually or emotionally. On the contrary, they are all too ready to form warm, comradely groups to the exclusion of women: sports clubs, monasteries, expeditions, scientific collaborations, TRADE UNIONS.

They are competitive yes. But on the whole much better than when with women: sense of competing is inferior.

13 MAY 1979: *Miscarriage.* It began as pain in left side. An ache, very near the pelvic cavity, and loss of libido. Dr H.'s pregnancy test was negative (only just), but some days later it was positive. Spotting and 'period pain' aches. I requested that my coil be removed. Refused by GP. I was bleeding more and waking in middle of night with prototype contractions—i.e. all lower stomach muscles hard and contracted.

Friday, the eleventh: told GP. She said wait till Monday. Saturday the twelfth: bleeding a lot. I had a tense talk with Mum for an hour. Around elevenish I had a bath to relax. For nearly a week and a half now I had been having full pregnancy nausea. When I got out of the bath, a clot of blood fell out of my vagina—about five tablespoons of it. No gushing. Shock of realization made me on point of fainting, while boyfriend phoned for an ambulance. Came round, retching, but only bitter saliva came up although I had had a pizza three hours before.

Ambulance came. I was over the shock. They took my blood pressure in ambulance. I think it was normalish. At hospital the doctor gave me a very uncomfortable internal examination, and I became tense again. The pressure made me shake. I went to the loo and felt as though my innards were falling out and indeed I discovered that I had left two large chunks of fibrous clots, like small bits of liver. Pain still on left side. Gripping aching pain that night, but quite bearable (possibly because of relaxation of bath). Registrar examined me at nine-thirty. On the thirteenth, my left side was still tender, and I was warned of a possible ectopic pregnancy, and permission was requested to make incision and look. Permission granted by me.

No pain to mention. Certainly not as bad as my period pains which are mild anyway. No temperature to mention. No blood pressure to mention—i.e. hospital thought I had fabricated story —which put me under considerable psychological pressure—until I again passed chunks of flesh. Refused pain-killers. No ectopic pregnancy. Considerable pain now: more restive-making than unbearable.

To All Cultural Papas

I must take a knife before I can paint a picture.
I thought I could do it without:
an impressionistic sweep of sand,
a finger pressed against the jugular and
a man running lopsidedly beside the water.
No dice.
Property of the Master.
Hunting Rights Strictly Reserved.
I shall need to force you
to be generous; to spend time in courting you
to kill you. With the vigours of a corpse
in your preventative forearm

you still hold keys that are mine.

Everywhere—in every conversation
you have hallowed me with the curse of
myself as art form. Nothing, you implied,
could match the lyric of sycophancy that
you fished for in my eyes.
You wanted me lover and model so you could murder me
friend.
You applauded my hesitations and
the elegant deference with which I shat on myself—
me and my mute lover gazed at each other—
and beyond you
I saw your brothers applauding you.

So to all you tired young male writers
who for want of talent or imagination
string up your hapless girlfriends in your verse
and prostitute yourselves again, in public,
I recommend the knife.

Thoughts. Dr Casement: can you *begin* to see how frightened I've been and how drugged? I need compassion, trust, detachment, calm.

Couldn't read *Lolita* (couldn't bear to). Just asked people what it was about. Only managed to find strength to read it six months ago. I was (*literally*) freaked. Blank. Then *anger*.

'Don't ever do that to me again'—told Pa without words. Said it again to the doctor at the Whittington: 'Don't *ever* do that to *anyone ever* again.'

Gerald Duckworth was a sod (just swearing).

At what point did I feel secure enough to re-integrate? Around the age of fifteen: HORROR. BLANK. No. I'm not ready. I'm not strong enough. I need more time and experience and help. I'm not fully integrated in myself yet. Tricky but interesting.

He loved to listen to my unconscious and then manoeuvre to

keep it in check. Now I can't open my mouth. When I look in a mirror I see a rat. Which is my internalized image of my father's image of me. He turned my own face against me. I keep on holding my hand over my mouth.

My dad wants me to believe I'm a walking unconscious. In fact he has just stunned one part of my mind and overdeveloped another. I need to find out more.

Art with a capital F: dear dear Father.

I was feeding the cats and striding about thinking how was I going to support them. And they kept on getting under my feet and I was saying, 'Don't get in my way, don't get in my way,'—as though it were a mantra. And then Bod—complacently thinking himself king-pin of the three (my father I see now) got under my feet one further time, and I gave him a death-blow. He sensed it momentarily but then forgot it. Ditto me. Now he has to suppress his anger because he wants to fly at me. I'm trying to find outlets for him (hunting, destroying moths, etc). This was around the time of my last abortion (I can't call it termination now for some reason—I know why: termination is death; abortion's a mess). There have been four abortions, approximately, and one miscarriage.

The Mask. I feel that my sexuality has been turned into the mask. Father 'tells' me directly and not so directly that sex is about sadism. (Homosexuality is *not* about sadism because the partners are equal and friends.) My childish question is why is heterosexual sex about sadism? My malevolent (frightened) father's answer is because women's sexuality is too frightening and disgusting not to be punished by men. I'm fighting that idea with everything in me but my father is blocking my efforts.

Heterosexual sex is out for me. So, too, is lesbianism. Flirtation is the only way I have of keeping my sane sexuality (and it *is* positive) alive. Therefore gay men (who make up many of my friends at the moment) are ideal because I can flirt to my heart's content without threat from them or to them.

I feel as though I'm walking a tightrope supporting an elephant. I can't carry anyone else's fears; I have enough to

69

contend with of my own.

My father has to call me a monstrosity—which makes him one to me. Because he hates himself so much he's desperately trying to push this self-hatred on to me (women generally is the pattern). I'm strong but I'm too vulnerable to cope. I need someone who can help me find my strength to dissolve what he's set up in me and to dissolve it in him without destroying him.

I have a different task. I need to sort out reality and myth to have a hold on them instead of vice versa as they do now, but I also have to play-act out of my system a fantasy of what I feel has gone wrong with me. This means I have at once to be reasonable and unreasonable, and the strain of holding these two contradictory features in balance and not falling apart is tremendous.

I feel very threatened by the fact that my father is sleeping with women who are my age or younger. I feel he is committing a kind of mental incest and that it is a message to me as his favourite daughter.

17 MAY 1979: As I can't love the feminine in women—I'll love it in men. And vice versa: I'll love the masculine in women.

My name: 'Sappho'. What is its reality? Its double reality? One more cross to bear *for which I hadn't been prepared by my parents* (sense of outrage). A name that encourages everyone to think I am a lesbian. On the other hand I know that sometimes I have almost consciously encouraged it: that tepid infatuation with the German girl who looked like the female counterpart to the guy I was obsessed by.

More bits of the picture of my father from my mother. When she managed to get him to talk about his early life he said that he could remember being born! He went into detail (which it was painful for him to tell) about how he was bruised and thrown away on a pallet for dead while they looked after 'that woman', his mother. He remembers that his head hurt badly and that he felt incredibly angry when, after they had seen to her, they came over to him and pulled his legs and slapped him on the back.

He talked about his relationship with his father only after my mother had threatened to leave (to charm her in some manner). At first he said he couldn't remember anything. My mum said that that was nonsense. Had he cared for his father? My dad said yes. Why then, my mother asked, did he always refer to him in terms that made him sound like an enemy? He wasn't an enemy, my father said, just a stranger. It was very painful trying to talk to him, my father said. But: he remembered one wonderful thing. When he was around eight or nine (his father died when he was twelve), his father took him aside and asked him seriously what he wanted to become when he was an adult, and my father told him he wanted to be a poet. His father had said that in that case he would send him to all the right schools in order to give him the necessary training—which he did to the best of his knowledge, being himself an engineer. I think that this incident was what he *wanted* his father to have done, but not what actually happened. My mother says that my grandmother made all the decisions in the family and that she was fixated to an unhealthy degree on the children (her province for power) and unconsciously cut the husband out. Apparently my grandmother and grandfather couldn't go out to parties because she would go into a tizz and insist on getting back as soon as possible to make sure that the children were all right. She never ever made friends—the family was everything to her. My grandfather was redundant long before he died.

I told my mother that I thought that my grandmother had hated me and was never more than indifferent to me. My mother said that until the split-up it was exactly the reverse—my grandmother had doted on me and spoilt me out of all proportion, just as she had her own children.

I remember the 'fateful choice' scene as a simple choice between my mother and father with my grandmother in the wings. In fact the real scene according to my mother was very different. What started out as a minor wrangle over the question of washing my hair turned into a fully blown haggle for control over me—and my father, grandmother and me were all lined up against my mother while they told her that she was a disruptive influence and she was upsetting me and making me do things that

71

I didn't want to do and that she would turn me into a neurotic (!). My father and grandmother suggested that she should give me up and go. I was, apparently, holding my grandmother's hand and I disentangled myself and said, 'I want to do what Mummy tells me to do,' and my grandmother flew into a complete temper and pushed me towards my mother saying, 'Go to your mother if you want to.'

My mother said that something strange used to happen whenever my grandmother and I got out of the house and went visiting. I would suddenly come out with a cutting remark about my mother, speaking as though I were my father and fully adult. It was so uncanny that even my grandmother was shaken by it and apologized to my mother, saying, 'I'm sorry my dear. I don't understand this.' My mother was in such a bad state that she just thought this was one more thing meant to unsettle her and she's blanked out what I said, but remembers that it was as if I were mirroring the worst aspects of my father and just coughed them up—as though to confirm his presence among us. She never mentioned this to my father but thinks that Granny did because it was so eerie.

31 MAY 1979: CASEMENT'S INVOICE. Thirteen sessions during May: £140.

1 JUNE 1979: 9 a.m. Leg wax. 12 p.m. Casement. Evening: Charlie Chaplin's *Gold Rush*. Remember being fascinated and watching till the last minute. Actually was screaming and had to be carried out.

Sappho was a regular correspondent with her father. The following letter from her, dated 14 June 1979, is in response to a letter she received from him, in which he urges her to approach her psychoanalysis sessions properly—not to waste money, but to view them with seriousness and get on top of her 'rat-like super-ego.' Her trouble, he says—this 'angustia', this 'angst'—is due to a physical shock and not neurosis, 'though you may have another kind of phobic thing underneath.' He signs the letter 'Lover'.

Dearest Pa

Many thanks for the lovely letter. The only bit I didn't like was the unkind reference to my 'rat-like super-ego'. I shall cross swords with you for that you old fart![1] As for psychoanalysis: you may be right but I'm playing it entirely by ear. At the moment everything has stabilized out and I feel a lot lighter.[2]

We seem to be in for some traditional spring weather here for a change now that the Conservatives are back with their Good Goddess rain-bearing Maggie. Pudding Island has signed its death pledge and it's toy-town all the way to the grave, I fear. Maybe not.

I'm having fun welding my Brontë sketches together. Branwell is something of a tough nut because he comes across so much (in researches) as a joke figure. But then there are two versions of him (of course) and in EJB's mind something else rather interesting is going on. Him on himself: the scene something of a cross between 'The Death of Chatterton' and Tambi's hotel room in Avignon. Icy order of the sisters all around his chaos.[3] 'They've even pared off my toenails for fear that they should turn into wings or I slit my throat on them!' I've got some good morbid sub-EJB songs for this great woman. At any rate such play should get some of the 'heaving passions' off my chest. (You remember Fuseli's *Nightmare*?) But this is all pap until I get on to some more serious stuff.[4]

---

[1]Sappho re-wrote letters to her father until she arrived at the version she was happy to send. The annotations below were made on one of these earlier drafts (although after the final version was mailed). Here, Sappho writes after the sentence, *I shall cross swords with you for that you old fart*: 'CALLING HIS CARD.'

[2]After the sentence, *At the moment everything has stabilized out and I feel a lot lighter*, she writes, 'PUTTING HIM AT REST. I'M NOT CONTINUING.'

[3]After the sentence, *Icy order of the sisters all around his chaos*, she writes, 'HIS BLUFF CALLED.'

[4]After the sentence, *But this is all pap until I get on to some more serious stuff*, she writes, 'I AM PUTTING FEAR IN HIM.'

At the moment am enamoured of Richard Wilbur[5]—he should have got the poetry chair at Oxford but of course was an outsider because not involved in the genteel scrumming. He's an excellent craftsman—like Sotatsu: a fine line and extravagant content.[6]

Proof-reading a book called *Animals are my Best Friends* (the truth guv!) ghost-written for the Director of the Dublin Zoo in such sub Gerry (yes, it *is* possible)—stroke—Irish whimsy that the Director himself felt moved to scoop some off with a trowel — insisting on drastic readjustments so that he could hold his head up in the Dublin bars.[7] Oh these small delights. Almost as touching as A L Rowse's subconscious—but not quite.[8]

I shall know when I feel better: when I feel able to face Bernard Stone and all that awful millpond again. There's a good Geiger-counter.

Give us a ring to let us know how things are going *chez toi*. Will so ditto. When do you get back from Greece?[9] I wouldn't mind coming down for a stay in Sommières circa mid-September (which is when I'm free of this literary agent work).

LOTSA LOVE, AS ALWAYS

Saph

---

[5]She writes, 'CONSCIOUS, DELIBERATE SLIP TO TEST HIM OUT. ACTUALLY A U.S. POET. HE OBVIOUSLY DOESN'T KNOW HIM.'

[6]After *a fine line and extravagant content*, she writes, 'DADA IN SWITCH ROUND. NABOKOV.'

[7]After *insisting on drastic readjustments so that he could hold his head up in the Dublin bars*, she writes, 'FRIGHTENED HIM INTO STITCHES WHICH IS WHY HIS CONSCIOUS LEASH SLIPPED AND HE SIGNED HIS LETTER "LOVER".'

[8]She writes, 'ME TRYING TO SAY I FORGAVE HIM. HE'S NOT SURE I HAVE THOUGH BECAUSE HE CAN'T CONCEIVE OF ANYBODY EVER FORGIVING HIM. HE'D BREAK UNDER THE STRAIN.'

[9]She writes, 'HE CAN'T GO TO GREECE THIS SUMMER BECAUSE HE'S PARALYSED IN FRANCE TRYING TO STOP MY LANGUAGE (FRENCH).'

16–17 JUNE 1979: *Cold Turkey weekend*. Mr Casement—I shall always make the distinction between you as analyst and you as benevolent father-figure. If you're worried (when you're worried) prompt me or ask me and I shall make the distinction.

In any event, you'll do. I'm desperate. Welcome to my pantheon.

I'm terrified of men. All their energy has gone wrong on them. Why don't they let women help? Some women can see and help.

All those dead months I have to make up in hours of tears.

Gay men—I'm attracted to anyone who's really traumatized by sexuality as I am—and as I'm heterosexual it has to be men.

The prostitutes and the women he sleeps with who are my age or younger and yet he is so wearingly puritanical (and prurient) about female sexuality. A creep.

Two fathers and one wants to kill me.

That man's subconscious has just run amok.

I'm terrified. He's going to commit suicide and he's trying to take me with him. *Livia, or Buried Alive*. Suttee/puttee.

Love I can't cope with. Pain and anger I can.

Malevolent and benevolent father. Not a hard and fast rule but just a way of dealing with the contradictions in his character.

Love him but don't trust him (Father).

When I mentioned pains in chest he was almost content! Wittering on about how I was going to share heart complaints with Pinky.

He wants me to suffer in retribution. He can't see I'm almost insensible already. Monstrous ego.

I'm an active person who's been bludgeoned into being passive to survive (though the strain is killing me now).

Mantra during early adolescence: I'm dead. Mantra during mid-adolescence: I don't exist.

As an adult I can't survive with my father. If I'm a woman (wife) he has to destroy me like all his wives because he has to kill what he loves; and if I'm a man I'm a rival and therefore he has to destroy me.

I want to be able to have enough confidence in myself to stop watching myself and get on with living.

Men's bodies make me blank and vaguely disgusted because I associate them with pain and confusion and violence. And I am over my head in anger that a scraggy piece of meat can allow a person to behave like a prostitute and still think themselves a god.

Night-dress—blood batik/batik in blood.

Pa doesn't like me because I can play him at his own game (*vide*: 'don't wring your hands too much, that's my advice to an actor.' That made him sit up).

My mind's coming back.

Desperate to sort out reality and illusion but have yet to act out fantasy.

Male look of fear: 'Good God she's got a pair of false teeth between her legs.' Why are they so frightened by women's sexuality? Because their guilt rises to heaven—what they have done to women's sexuality and self-determination fills them with repressed guilt.

He gave me the key and then marked me. Showed me heaven and hell in an instant.

Before you sink yourselves in erroneous love remember that Sappho was a bisexual. I smoke only Gauloises: is it because of the Hermes sign on the packet or is it because it reminds me of Claude?

Story set in Israel where women were raped etc. by Roman soldiers. A soldier raped this woman and then knocked out her teeth so that she'd never be attractive again and be able to make love to anyone. (It repulses me, but the victim in me is attracted. It fills me with unreasoning *rage*, as does reading about rape.)

His attitude to analysis is: 'you would pluck out the heart of my mystery'—he'd rather die/kill than that—for Art.

We had a standing joke in the family that his wine belly was actually because he was working on a false pregnancy—gestating novels—old man of the sea—Tiresias.

Most female literary models that I have for tradition died young or tragically: Sappho, Sylvia Plath, Emily Brontë, Dickinson(?), V Woolf.

Androgyny. Why? Because sexuality was impossible for me and I knew it? Very fat—especially just after Claude's death when I put on two stone. Compulsive eater. Passive. Running around in a stupor of desperation.

If I can swim clear of the wreck of my father . . .

I can see so he had to paralyse me (his subconscious). He knew I knew so he had to paralyse me. He's just enough of a confidant to seem like a friend but his subconscious is actually working against me. He feels guilty for something he did to me so he has to try and kill me.

I describe the shadowy figure and go into quandary: there is someone on foot on the stairs. A slight start. On me? Behind me?

I need to fall apart. I need to relax a little—*not to let him in* but to get him out.

Two flying dreams: The first was heaven. It was magic. I was flying using my arms like wings and the air somehow supported me as though like water but wasn't water. I flew round an antiquarian bookshop and then out over a green landscape to a grey castle. I flew up the wall, smashing it with my fists and everywhere water appeared and then turned into a torrent and gushed out. ('Who would smite the living fountains from the rocks along our way.') And then it started to flood and became a bit *threatening* (but all of it still euphoric). I rode away with some men on a horse.

I was on my own. I trusted myself. Smashing the castle: what I've been doing with Simon poor guy—trying to get him to cry

and that is precisely what he can't do because of his problems.*
He can't get me to cry.

Second flying dream. Bad. Flying in a plane with my father.
I told him that I was frightened of flying which gave his
subconscious the cue it needed. He tried to resist inducing
hysteria in me but finally had to succumb, having now turned me
from daughter into wife and Claude having become the belovèd
ghost. I'm 'bad'/real—as well as being the ungrateful daughter.
He's using Thomas Hardy poems to reinforce this in himself—to
hide himself from himself behind her pedestal.

The dream: we were breaking up eye pencils, grey and blue
to eat the 'lead'. I felt sick. The plane was Concorde and it
crashed though somehow I survived.

Androgyny is the only way I can survive and not be the object of
retribution. I must therefore constantly check that I am attractive
to both gay men and gay women with *no threat*. Apart from
compulsion it is great fun and appeals to my sense of
humour—piss-take of 'femininity' and 'masculinity' and the
concept of androgyny is to hold the two principles in balance.

Pa: he is absolutely cold, or else the miserable little tyrant of a
ten-year-old boy. He knows I've rumbled him. No light coming
from him or through him. Beauty is soul deep. What's happened
to him?

This guy has a mainline to my subconscious which he uses badly.
I have to kill him or be killed.

I left him a PS saying: 'FUCK FREUD! (and sod that if that's
a double-edged valediction!).' Freud = him / Laing = me, so he
phoned to reinforce my feelings of being a victim. I then felt a
pain in my chest and arms as a delayed reaction to coping with
the implications of his phone call. I danced to some music. I'm
carrying my father's life—I have a responsibility for it—as his
wife. His subconscious knows that and is going to use it against
me any way possible.

---

*Simon Tompsett and Sappho Durrell married in 1980 but
spent most of their marriage separated.

20 JUNE 1979: CASEMENT'S INVOICE. Thirteen sessions in June: £149.

24 JULY 1979: Two fathers. How much do you know about depressions arising from incest as vs *mental* trauma? Oedipal. Existential depression, yes but I suspect more than just that. Wouldn't have been able to know enough about my problems to ask you this question when I last saw you.

26 JULY 1979: Casement: it has become crucial that you don't budge an inch and that you aren't rattled—even though my subconscious is showing signs of transferring and it is necessary for me *at this stage* to transfer on to a 'homosexual' father. Bear with me. I feel that you are blocking me from saying things because you can't bear to hear them.

You don't want to hear certain things about my father or to consider them deeply because they strike a chord in you of something that you should have resolved and come to terms with and so you are trying to shield him. Defector. And you are trying to get me to protect both him and you against the truth in yourselves. I can only protect one—and that is the one who is my real father—he's suicidal and you're not and I love him and I don't love you. However, as we can both see, I need to transfer subconsciously on to you—but I can *see* that. So I am going to be quite open and honest about it. This means that you must resolve your fears about (a) female sexuality, (b) your own homosexuality, (c) male brutality so that you can be solid enough to cope with a subconscious transference that you find extremely threatening.

Up to now I've been saying things obliquely and slowing myself down in places to protect you. This is insane—I shouldn't be feeling that I have to protect you—the reverse should be true. You're anxious to protect yours and my father's guilt (actually his is very different from yours) from my exposure. Face yourself and then you can face my father and you needn't block me.

My problem is with men and therefore must be worked out with a man—to test out reality *vs* illusion.

Thank you for using some of the things thrown up during the 'cold turkey' weekend to help things along.

You've brought out the megalomaniac in me.

Lawrence Durrell's next letter to his daughter continues from the last, offering more observations about the nature of psychoanalysis, the importance of Freud, but also the shortcomings: 'Fortunately the system, though marvellous . . . is very limited.' Even so, she will have some fun and a chance to release some of her stress. Her current troubles, he informs her, have less to do with Freudian neurosis than with the fact that she has been 'trying to grow a prick in the wrong place': what in the old days would have been called a 'masculine protest', when it was understood that the girls who were worried about not having penises grew moustaches. He offers the example of other 'phallocrats': Mrs Scott Fitzgerald and Mrs Dylan Thomas. Men also, he concedes, 'worry themselves into stitches about not having wombs'—it is not only a female problem—and, in men, the protest erupts in bumps, goitres and cancers. He mentions an operation he has had himself to remove 'two large lumps of camel fat off my back.' His letter is re-typed by Sappho and covered with annotations. These are some:

'*Fortunately* the system, though marvellous . . . is very limited': MEANS UNFORTUNATELY.

LENGTHY AND EMBARRASSING DISCURSIVE PIECE OF HIS USING MRS DYLAN THOMAS AND MRS SCOTT FITZGERALD AS E.G.s . . . YUK!

CANCERS IN STRATEGIC PLACES: DIVERSION ON CYST OPERATION JUST HAD.

'Men also worry themselves into stitches': MY VERSION OF HIS MESSAGE: I'M SO FRIGHTENED AND SADDENED BY MYSELF

AND WHAT I'VE DONE I WANTED TO DIE.
FORGIVE ME.

31 AUGUST 1979: CASEMENT'S INVOICE. seven sessions: £80.50.

30 SEPTEMBER 1979: CASEMENT'S INVOICE. ten sessions: £115.

3 OCTOBER 1979: Amazing how a journal gives one a sense of going somewhere. Necessary for self-employed on intangible pursuits. Byron, even with an ego like his, needed to record for any voice (his own) who would listen: 'read—rode—shot pistols—dined—talked nonsense—went to bed' or some such. I'll try it as a chest-expander. Some earlier stuff has already fallen apart (necessary in what I'm going through) but that's no reason now to hang fire on trying again.

13 OCTOBER 1979

In the event of my death: *it is my wish* that my part in the house 39, Loraine Road, London N7 and all my books and possessions shall pass to my mother, Mrs Eve Durrell, presently of 27e St James's Gardens, W11, and, if not her, through some eventuality, then to Mr Simon Tompsett of 39, Loraine Rd, N7. *I'm sound in mind and body* as my writing will testify. [I would like the Robson children to have any mementoes that my mother feels to be appropriate, including art books and catalogues. I should like, if possible, to be buried in Steep churchyard. Any dream notebooks (mostly in the attic), where appropriate, can be shown to Mr Casement. In the event that my father should request to be buried with me—my wish is that the request be refused. (6.7.81)]

Sappho Durrell

16 OCTOBER 1979
Ms Judith Herman
c/o The Sciences
The New York Academy of Science

ˈDear Ms Herman

I read with great interest yours and Ms Hirschman's article in *The Sciences* on the subject of Father/Daughter Incest and its attendant consequences.

I gather from asking psychologists and psychiatrists over here that relatively little work has been done on this particular problem and this impression is strongly borne out by the tenor of your article. Then again, the US seems to be well ahead of Europe and the UK in researching or indeed correlating incidences of this form of abuse.

I am at present preparing an article to submit to the feminist magazine *Spare Rib* on the long and short-term psychological effects of this and I would be extremely grateful to know of any recent books, research papers, or of people working in this field either here or in the States.

I look forward to hearing from you in the near future,
Yours sincerely
Ms Vivien Gantry *

29 OCTOBER 1979: CASEMENT'S INVOICE. Seven sessions in October: £80.50.

20 NOVEMBER 1979
READING LIST:
Patterns of Incest, Julian Press, NY, Masters W. H. and Johnson V.E., 1976.

British Journal of Sociology, 5, pp 101-17, 1984.

Conspiracy of Silence, Sandra Butler, Bantam Press, 1978.

Sexual Assault of Children and Adolescents, D. C. Heath, Boston, 1978.

---

*Sappho Durrell's pseudonyms included Vivien Gantry, Frances Duarte and Mr Latimer.

Incest, K. Meiselman, Josselyn-Bass, 1978.

Women in Between, Marilyn Strathern, Semina Press, 1972.

Incest, Herbert Maisch, (Translated from German), 1965.

26 NOVEMBER 1979: CASEMENT'S INVOICE. Four sessions in November: £46.

30 JANUARY 1980
Dear Enquirer

The booklet on how to end one's life has not yet been written but when it is available, in about three months, we shall inform all members.

The booklet will only bc available to members.

I therefore enclose details about the Society, and hope you decide to join.

Yours sincerely
Nicholas Reed
General Secretary
Exit—The Society for the Right to Die with Dignity

30 JANUARY 1980
Dear Ms Durrell

Thank you for your cheque for £23 in payment for the weekend February 15–17. (I am assuming that you are the same person as Vivien Gantry.) We are expecting you from Friday p.m. until Sunday tea at 4 p.m. Supper is served at 6.30 p.m. on Friday.

With every good wish,
Yours sincerely
Mrs D Lederman (Secretary)
The Order of Carmelites
Retreat and Conference Centre
Allington Castle
Maidstone
Kent

11 JUNE 1980
Dear Pa

It was good to hear you on the phone. I shall probably be able to get away around the end of August for a couple of weeks, and may travel down with some friends of mine who are on their way to India via Greece.

I hope you will be there, because it makes absolutely no sense for me to flog down to Sommières unless you are. Hope all is well.

LOTSA LOVE
Saph

30 JUNE 1980: CASEMENT'S INVOICE. Three sessions in June: £34.50.

16 JULY 1980
Dear Pa

It was good to hear you yesterday and reassuring to know that you are well. (You've become such a crusty old badger with me that it's hard for me, what with nervousness and the sort of semaphore we speak over the phone, to assess how you are.) So.

Please put aside *at least one* evening between the 18th Sept and 2nd Oct to come and have a slap-up, boozy supper *chez nous*.

The garden is looking very fine so it would be good if it was at a weekend and we could have a kebab lunch outside for starters, Retsina and all—or whatever.

If Anthea's pals' flat falls through, *par hasard*, you are more than welcome to stay here if you can stand to 'rough it' (and I *mean* rough—wait till you see us: we have just knocked down a major wall and are knee-high in plaster dust, and the place is a bit like a Bedouin encampment). But we'd be delighted to have you stay and, as soon as we're straightened out more here, that's an invitation which will have more allure for you than at present.

Opposite: Lawrence Durrell

Photo: Mark Gerson

I hope that Athens was, as the Americans say, a 'gas' (details of the prize got lost in telephone crackle. Which work was it for?).

Lots of love and looking forward to seeing you again soon,
Saph

(PS I wish you would bury your six hatchets once and for all and sound a *little* bit pleased to hear from me when I phone. Do I have to spell out how much it all upsets me?) Lotsa love—S

31 JULY 1980
Dear Mr Casement,

Herewith a cheque for £69 with many thanks.

It worried me not a little that you seemed under the impression that I might still have some contact with the Maudsley.* I have absolutely no contact with the Maudsley and have no reasons (after my one interview) to have contact.

To clarify: my reasons for going to the Maudsley on my *own* behalf were *un*conscious and semiconscious fears about lack of containment because I'd heard that they had a container for unresolved and excessive feelings of violence, the 'smash and grab room'. As you know already, I find it extremely difficult not to feel profoundly pessimistic about *anything* being an adequate container for my problems. The situation for me, as compared to this time last year, is very different, as it is one that has been fully tested, and I don't feel any necessity to repeat last year's little performance when you went on holiday.

As for funds, I hope to be into a slightly better paid job soon so that I can begin proper analysis, by the time you get back. And if not, then I'm prepared to wait until I am in such a position.

Have a good holiday.
With very best wishes,
Sappho Durrell

---

*The Maudsley Hospital for psychiatric treatment is in South London.

Sappho's letter below is in response to one from her father dated 12 October 1980. It would appear that from September the previous year Sappho suffered some kind of nervous breakdown. Her father's letter expresses his relief that she has finally regained her good health and attributes her illness to having to re-enact and exorcise her mother's 'ancient breakdown' (the one that occurred shortly after Sappho was born). He closes his letter describing his dream of an ideal woman—Durrell is having to do his own cooking and cleaning and mailing of parcels. She would be a mixture of Madame Mignot and Xanthippe who will hold him upright in his tub and feed him while he 'Diogenises'.

Dear Pa

At last a moment to sit down and write you a fulsome thankyou for your lovely warm letter. I am relieved that everything physical is ticking over nicely. Your asthma can be eased away with yoga (she says blithely). Certainly you looked in the pink of reassuring health when you were in London. Most probably (models after 1945 having built-in obsolescence) you are in better health than I am. I've given up nurturing the hectic flush on my left cheek.

(It was also heartening to get a warm response last Sunday. Here's hoping that this last week was fruitful and some good work has come of it.)

Simon and I are in the last stages of disembowelling the downstairs rooms to make one L-shaped living-room and have plaster dust all over again. Us and the cats coughing and sneezing our way around and dredging bits of lath out of our tea (not the cats . . .). I am soon rid of two of the three cats. This will rank as Bliss in the First Degree. One self-important cat is absolutely adequate for me. (Simon is also relieved.)

O where are you going to find this good woman? Is none of your beautiful American correspondents going to prevent you wasting away? (What an awful paradox in the land of plenty.) Incidentally, attended an *absolutely magical* concert of eleventh–thirteenth century music: troubadour songs and poems; Bernart de Ventadorn, Jaufre Rudel de Blaye, Marcabru, Guillaume de

Machaut, Gace Brule, Guilhem IX, Guirat Riquier, Mermot d'Arras. With luck I may be able to make a recording of it as it is being broadcast here in November. The sounds ranged from those akin to delicate Indian Ragas to Irish peasant ballads (no surprise in this, but it was a delightful, spirited performance throughout, as well). Funny, memorable, haunting. All in Provençal with intermittent translations here and there. Fingers crossed for a recording. Anthea is coming to supper tomorrow, and I'm afraid the place is like a skip. Never mind. One must chuckle.

Lots of love. Keep up the good work, and for goodness sake don't waste away. I hope that Xmas here wouldn't disperse you too much. See how you feel nearer the time. I have my free days booked (a certain amount of crude arm-twisting here) with some difficulty, so you'd better, or else . . . by then we shall have a workable spare room if Les Brontës cannot materialise.

In any event, lots of love and look after yourself. Will write again when I have a moment. Good and happy novelling—
Saph

31 OCTOBER 1980: CASEMENT'S INVOICE. Five sessions in October: £57.50.

27 NOVEMBER 1980: CASEMENT'S INVOICE. Four sessions in November: £46.

17 DECEMBER 1980: CASEMENT'S INVOICE. Three sessions in December: £34.50.

23 JUNE 1981: Yes—I'll say it again. I am sick of the inside of men's minds. Of all their unnecessary inhumane self-centred garbage; of the sound of them trundling their smelly little snot-coloured egos around in their heads like dung beetles—or like boys whipping tops to make themselves seem more lively or more fascinating. Top to bottom, east to west—men—because of their self-absorption and adulation—have become garbage. Sad. Only exceptions are some poets and some homosexuals.

Ones I've met are mulch. Bitter bitter bitter thoughts about Simon.

13 JULY 1981
Dear Pa

Thank you for a delightful refreshing week. I wish it could have been for longer. Back in shabby London where the weather is strangely thundery and hot. I shall get the Schopenhauer pamphlet to you in the course of the next week or so. Incidentally, the novel I mentioned to you is by Salman Rushdie and is called *Midnight's Children*. The Mozart *Cosi Fan Tutte* recording which you will enjoy (if it's still in print) is by Karl Böhm with Elizabeth Schwarzkopf *et al* and is a genuine delight—funny, sad, triumphant. Keep me posted on news and let me know in advance of any change of plans.

    LOTS OF LOVE, of course
    Saph

15 NOVEMBER 1981
Dear Pa

A swift note of thanks for the hello—albeit I must confess that my heart sank at cheques, and scribbled messages on press cuttings and forwarded letters.* Back to old times. Even so, many thanks.

    Lots of love
    Saph
    PS: I loathe addressing you at *poste restante*. (It makes it sound as though you own the flippin' island!)

---

*The package from her father contained, like many previous ones, a large collection of press clippings and reviews about his work, correspondence, some of it intimate, from friends and other members of the family, and a number of love letters from admirers.

Sappho Durrell

10 JULY 1982
T207
c/o *Time Out*
Southampton Street
London WC1

Dear T207,

Sounds appealing. My particular interests are theatre, poetry, cinema, psychology, writing (including free-lance reviewing) as well as classical and some contemporary music, dance, some opera (not Bel Canto . . . though) etc.

I'm 31, attractive, talented (she says), solvent and an English Literature graduate, North London based, separated. You didn't mention your age so perhaps I ought to say here that with older men (over 40) it remains friendship only . . .

If you think that our interests and personalities might tally then phone me at 607 6154 (after 6 p.m.) and we could meet on neutral ground.

Yours sincerely
Vivien Gantry

On the night of 31 January 1985, Sappho Durrell hanged herself by a rope fixed to the skylight in the attic room of her house. She was discovered the next morning by one of her lodgers, after he broke open the door. Her life was declared extinct at 12.10 p.m. on 1 February 1985. Her suicide note, originally dated 24 January 1985 but crossed out and corrected, was written to her mother. It mentions a fifth abortion and the fear of another nervous breakdown and asks that certain relatives be kept at a distance from her writings and her belongings.

Sappho Durrell was buried in Trent Park cemetery in London under the name of Sappho Jane Tompsett née Durrell.

Overleaf: Sappho Durrell

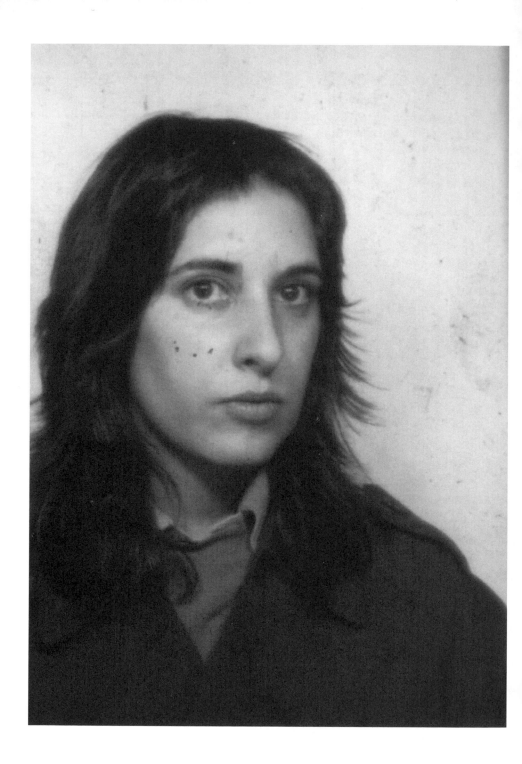

WILLIAM WHARTON
FIELD BURNING

WWill and I push our bikes along the narrow alley between the house and the fence of the house next door. We're dripping wet from a three-mile run we've just made in Asbury Park. The run is every Thursday evening at seven on the boardwalk and conducted by the local YMCA. We've ridden the mile or so from there back home. The air is soft and soothing.

Rosemary, my wife, is already home. She'd driven back. We've invited good friends who run with us to eat at our house. She's come home to set the table and put things out. Albie and Linda, with whom we run on Monday and Thursday evenings, are stopping to get the pizza. Bobbie, another friend who is joining us, is with them. Will, our younger son, and I have enjoyed riding slowly through the darkening evening and look forward to showers and good pizza with friends.

As I push my bike past the dining-room window, I just catch the movement of Rosemary coming back through the kitchen. I park my bike near the trash cans. Will parks his along the fence leaning over the marigolds we've planted. He rushes in past Rosemary to get his shower started so I can have mine after him. I figure I'll help with anything Rosemary needs.

She pauses on the little covered back porch, on the platform outside the kitchen door. I'm just stepping over the little sill into the porch when she comes quickly down the steps to me. It's enough out of the ordinary that I take notice. I see she's crying.

She comes into my arms. I hold her tight. She's sobbing so hard I can feel it through her whole body and mine. I think, what in heaven's name can be wrong, Rosemary is not an easy crier. I'm just beginning to think about all our loved ones, mostly the few older aunts and uncles who are left. Then she looks up, takes my head in both her hands, stares into my eyes. I can scarcely make her out in the dark.

'Bert, darling, a terrible thing has happened.'

She stops to take a deep stuttering breath.

'They're all dead. Bill, Kate, Mia, Dayiel. They're all dead. I just finished talking to Betty Rodewald. They were killed in a huge crash and fire on the highway in Oregon. They're dead.'

She leans her head into my sweaty shoulder and cries hard some more. I hold on to her, as much to keep myself up as anything. I'm surprised at my reaction. I don't believe it. Somebody's made a mistake. I can't accept it. All the usual reactions people have to things they don't want to believe. But I'm not crying. I've just started shaking my head against Rosemary's.

'When did it happen? How? Are you sure?'

She talks into my shoulder. 'It happened yesterday at about four o'clock Oregon time. There was a fire that blew across the road. Seven people were killed. About thirty cars piled up. Betty was crying so hard it was hard to understand. I still don't understand.' Betty Rodewald is my daughter's mother-in-law.

'It happened yesterday? Are you sure? What took so long? What kind of people won't even tell you right away when something like this happens?'

'I wish it weren't true. They're dead.'

I hold her tighter. I'm beginning to shiver. I feel cold all the way inside myself. How could this happen? These are the kinds of things that happen to other people. We've always been so lucky. Bill, Kate's husband, is such a careful driver; Kate, even more so. She won't go around the block in a car with the babies unless they're strapped into baby seats, like astronauts, with wide straps crossed over them.

I turn Rosemary and lead her back up the steps into the kitchen. She's slumped against me. I'm still not crying. It hasn't registered yet. I hear the Jeep pulling in, parking out front. I lead Rosemary into the living-room, ease her into the reclining chair where she likes to read in the evenings.

Our friends are standing on our front porch. I open the door. They're wearing jackets against the chill after the run. Albie is holding the grease-stained paper box with the pizza out with two hands. He's smiling, the women are behind him. They know right away something has happened; something is wrong.

'We've just had some terrible news.'

For the first time I feel I might break down, crying. Telling it to someone else will make it more real, irrevocable.

'Kate, Bill, Mia and Dayiel have been killed in some kind of monstrous automobile accident in Oregon. Rosemary just phoned and talked to Bill's mom. It happened yesterday afternoon.'

95

Albie puts the pizza down on the table by the window.

'And they're only telling you now?'

It's the same reaction I had. Rosemary begins talking behind me. I know her. She doesn't want anyone thought badly of when they haven't done anything wrong.

'They didn't know themselves until just about an hour ago. It's only afternoon there. The accident was so horrible they couldn't identify the bodies for a long time. The Rodewalds were expecting them home for dinner last night. They didn't come. They thought the car had broken down or they'd decided to stay over with friends. The accident was on all the news, television, everything, all over the country, but they didn't think this kind of thing could happen to the family.'

She stops, leans forward with her face in her hands. Linda goes over, gets down on her knees, holds on to Rosemary. I'd better get off my feet or I'm going to fall down. I slump on to the floor with my head against the side of the couch, the way I watch baseball on television. Bobbie pulls some pillows off the couch and tucks them under my head. Both Linda and Bobbie are crying now. Each have children of their own.

Albie pulls my legs out straight, goes into the dining-room and brings out a chair. He lifts my legs up on to the chair; Bobbie puts another pillow under my legs. I guess from their reactions I must be going into shock. I know I feel terrible. I can't stop shaking my head back and forth, like a pendulum. It's totally involuntary.

Linda takes the pizza into the kitchen. She comes back with wet towels for both Rosemary and me. I'm beginning to feel as if things are passing me by. I want to comfort Rosemary but I'm numb. Albie is on his knees beside me now.

'Do you want me to get the first aid people? I can call them and they'll be here in five minutes.'

I shake my head no. It interrupts my regular rhythm of head shaking.

'No. I think we should just be alone for a while. I still have to tell Will. He doesn't know yet. We'll be all right. You people go home to your families.'

Rosemary sits up in her chair, ready to play hostess.

'Yes, please go home. We'll have many things to do. Nobody can do anything for us right now. If we do need help, we'll call.'

Bobbie leans towards Rosemary.

'I know I won't sleep tonight, so call any time, and I'll be right over. Dave can help, too. You know life-guards are trained in first aid. You don't need to take this all alone.'

Linda and Albie are standing. It's uncomfortable knowing they want to help, but all of us know there's nothing they can do. We just have to work it out ourselves.

They leave. I try to get them to take the pizza. No one feels like eating. I see them off the porch and into the Jeep. I look around at the quiet street in the night. Ocean Grove is famous for its peace. I wonder if it will ever be the same for me. I turn back into the house. I go over and kneel before Rosemary, take her hands in mine. Her crying has subsided.

I hear Will coming down the stairs. The stairs enter on to the dining-room. This house is three rooms in a row on the ground floor, living-room off front porch, then dining-room and kitchen in back. I stop Will at the bottom of the stairs.

'Will, I have something to tell you.'

Will is usually diffident. But he catches something in my voice, my face. Still he's carrying through what was for him the normal sequence.

'I left enough water for you to shower and there's still a dry towel.'

'Will, I have some bad news, something terrible has happened.'

He stands there, hanging his hands loosely at his sides. I wish I didn't have to say it. We could have let him have one more night's peaceful sleep. But it has to be done.

'Kate, Bill, Mia and Dayiel were killed in an automobile crash in Oregon. Mom just talked to Mrs Rodewald. That's how we found out.'

His face blanches. He stands there blank for a few seconds. He peers into the living-room.

'How's Mom taking it?'

'It's hard but she's OK.'

97

'Is there anything I can do?'

'Not now. Do you want some of the pizza? It's right there on the table.'

'No, I couldn't eat. I'll take a walk on the boardwalk. I don't think I can handle this.'

'Just be back before ten. I don't know when we'll be leaving for Oregon and the funeral. Probably tomorrow.'

'I'll be right back.'

I can tell he's on the edge of breaking down. I don't think I've heard him cry since he was under ten. I'm not interested in hearing it now. Walking along the boardwalk in the dark, crying, is more his style. He goes out the back door. I go into the living-room again. The running costume is looking more and more ridiculous. Then I remember that on Sunday we're supposed to be part of a big family reunion outside Philadelphia at my Aunt Alice's. I'll need to call. I also have to call my sister in California.

I slip off my warm-up jacket. It's beginning to dry on me. I slip off my soaking wet running shirt. I do these things automatically. I keep looking up at Rosemary. She's staring out of the window. I need to go upstairs to shower and put on some dry clothes but I don't want to leave her alone. I don't want to be alone either.

'Bert, you go on up and shower; I'm fine.'

She smiles. I smile back. We're being silly. Neither one of us expresses emotions easily.

I let the shower run over me for ten minutes. Here, I can cry. I wonder if Rosemary can cry downstairs. I dress in a pair of light slacks and a T-shirt, not exactly a mourning costume, but mourning costumes aren't our style either. I go down the steps slowly, preparing myself. Rosemary has moved from the chair by the window to the chair at the desk. She has the yellow pages in her lap and is talking on the phone. She hangs up.

'Well, we have a flight out of Newark for Portland, leaving at ten oh five tomorrow morning. We get to Portland at about noon. I'll call Betty Rodewald now and tell her what time we arrive. I think she told me the funeral is Tuesday. I'm not sure. I wasn't paying much atten—.' She breaks down. I go over and take her head to my chest. She puts her arms around my waist.

'Those beautiful young people. We're going to their funeral. It's all wrong.'

I hold her tighter and try to hold tight on to myself. I wonder how she got herself together enough to call the airlines. She amazes me. This is all a horror and a shock for me, but for her it must be impossible. Her life has been the kids. I have my painting and writing, other kinds of children in a way. But she's just lost her much loved first-born Kathleen, along with Bill and those two beautiful babies.

She gently pushes me away. She calls Betty Rodewald and tells her what time we hope to arrive. Bill's brother Steve will pick us up at the airport in Portland and drive us down.

'I guess we should call Camille,' she says.

I know the number by heart. It rings about ten times, then I hear Camille, sleepy-voiced, our only daughter now. I almost can't speak because the sobs are building up. It's three in the morning for her in France.

'Camille, this is Dad.'

I stop, take two deep breaths with my hand over the phone.

'Something terrible has happened.'

'What is it? Could you speak louder?'

I might as well get right into it. I don't have any choice. I'm sobbing as I say it.

'Kate, Bill, Dayiel and Mia were killed in an awful automobile crash in Oregon.'

'What?! Who told you that?'

I can't go on. Rosemary takes the phone. She's crying but not sobbing.

'I called to find out about Kate's gynaecologist appointment. I reached her little Wills, but Betty took the phone from him and she told me. It must be true. We can't believe it.'

I take the phone from Rosemary. Camille is crying, practically screaming. She's trying to tell Sam, her husband, what's happened. I say her name to get her attention.

'Camille.'

There's a long silence, then she says between sobs, 'I'm here.'

'Don't bother coming to the funeral. It's too far and Mom and I are sure we can handle it.'

'Whatever you say.'

That's not like Camille. She's generally against what *anybody* has to say. It's her way.

Rosemary moves into the kitchen and is unsetting the table she'd set for the pizza dinner. I go in and give her a hand. Twice, in passing, we stop, hug and hold on to each other. Neither of us can say anything.

Will comes in as we're finishing and goes straight upstairs and into his bedroom. Rosemary sits in the reclining rocker. Her face is swollen and red, her eyes swollen, too.

'We should probably pack tonight. There won't be much time in the morning.'

'Right, I'll tell Will.'

'Give him a little more time, first, dear. I know he'll be up late, he usually is. Just before we go to bed you can tell him about packing. Be sure to tell him to pack his suit, a shirt and a tie, extra socks and underwear.'

Going up the stairs behind Rosemary I'm reminded of Sisyphus, constantly climbing and falling back. We pull out a bag each and start. It all seems so unnecessary. I pack a charcoal-grey suit, the only real suit I own. I also have a summer suit but it needs cleaning. I throw in socks, underwear, a few changes of shirts, an extra pair of shoes, more dressy than the ones I'll wear on the plane. I peek over at Rosemary packing. She goes about it in her usual methodical way, folding carefully each dress, skirt, blouse, putting rubber bands around her stockings, underwear.

I go into the bathroom. I look dreadful. I splash water on to my face. I take four Valium out of the medicine cabinet, two for me and two for Rosemary. They're the yellow kind, five milligrams. I've never taken two before. I take one once in a while when I can't sleep. I hope two will be enough. I hope Rosemary will take hers. She doesn't like taking medicine of any kind, also has a terrible time swallowing pills.

We undress slowly, turn out the light and climb into bed. The French doors on to the porch are open, letting in a fresh ocean breeze. Then I remember I haven't taken my medication. I slide out of bed and go back into the bathroom. I take my pills for blood pressure and blood sugar, plus some others. I also remember I haven't told Will to pack.

On the way back to our bedroom, I knock at his door and open it. He's stretched out on his bed fully dressed. His eyes are red.

'Will, we're leaving so early in the morning you should pack before you go to sleep. Mom says be sure to pack your suit, a good white shirt and tie. Take along your best shoes, too. A funeral is an awfully formal kind of thing.'

'OK. But I don't think I'll sleep.'

'We're not sure we will either, but we're going to try. Tomorrow will be a long day, as will the next few days. So, get in your PJs and try to relax. If you want something to put you to sleep I have some pills.'

'Oh no, that won't be necessary.'

I back out of the room, shut the door. Will is the same as Rosemary when it comes to pills. I run downstairs and pull out the phone cord.

Our bed is basically two twin beds pushed together. We don't like to sleep apart but there's really no double bed in this house we rent every summer. I usually start out in Rosemary's bed and then as she falls asleep, roll over into the other bed, the bed by the French windows.

I close the bedroom door. Rosemary is stretched out on her back in her night-gown, but not under the covers. In summer, I sleep without pyjamas. I crawl across my bed to hers, snuggle in beside her and put my arm across her breast. She has her arms up over her head against the bedstead and one leg cocked up. She often begins sleep this way. Her eyes are open, tears are rolling slowly down her cheeks but there are no spasms of crying or sobbing. She's crying quietly to herself. I put my face against hers; her tears are cold. I can't think of anything to say. I don't really want to say anything but feel I should. Her voice seems so calm, so far away, so dry and emotionless, not like her at all.

'I never knew one's teeth could hurt so much from crying.'

'For me it's the ears, from trying not to cry. It's like the earaches I used to have when I was a kid. It hurts to swallow. Probably your teeth hurt from the same thing, trying to hold in;

you're biting down too hard.'

There's a long silence. We stay close. We spend an hour not moving, each pretending to sleep for the other. Finally, it's too much. I roll over to where I've put the pills and a glass of water. I turn back to Rosemary.

'I have some Valium. We really ought to sleep. Tomorrow's going to be tough.'

I hold out the pills. She doesn't move.

'I don't want to sleep. But you take something. Listen, Bert, do you really think we should go all the way to Oregon? They're dead, there's nothing we can do. Why don't we stay here where we were with them last and remember all the good times we had together. I know Kate wasn't sure I'd like Oregon. Most of the people there are roughnecks. Why don't we just keep it the way it is.'

I'm shocked. It seems so bizarre not going to the funeral of your own child, her husband and two of your only three grandchildren. I begin to wonder if Rosemary is all right. She's one for form, doing the proper thing. I keep quiet.

'Bert, if there are any bodies to see, I don't want to see them. They're probably terribly crushed and burned. I don't need that, neither do you. Why are we doing this?'

I went to my grandmother Wharton's funeral when I was nine, then to my grandfather's, my father's father, when I was fifteen. I was a pall bearer that time. Then there were the funerals for my mother and father, that's about it. That's a pretty good record for a man over sixty years old. I've been avoiding weddings and funerals all my life. In fact, I don't see much difference between the two. Rosemary knows this, I've said it often enough.

'All right, you're right, Rosemary. You know how I hate funerals. I'm sure if Kate and Bill can know what's going on, they'd agree with us. We haven't paid for any tickets so I'm sure we can cancel them. I can go in now and tell Will we're not going. I don't think that'll break his heart. I'll call our kids and tell them we're taking our own advice, staying home. If they want to go that's their business. What else? Boy, I feel better already.'

I roll out of bed to go in and tell Will.

'You're so sweet, darling. Don't. We *have* to go, there's just no way out of it, but as long as we both know that this entire farce is for others, that we don't need it, I feel better about things. I'm sorry I got your hopes up.'

I roll back on to my bed, take the glass of water and pop three Valium. Maybe we'll have a mass grave.

At first the pills don't work and I can tell Rosemary is still awake. My watch sounds midnight. I begin to think there shouldn't be anybody calling us between now and the time we leave unless it's our kids trying to get in touch. I roll quietly out of bed and go downstairs. I plug the phone back in.

The pills must have worked, finally, because when I come back up, I go out like a light. I wake to the ringing of the phone downstairs. I stagger across the foot of the bed. Rosemary is rolling out of her side.

'You go back to sleep dear, I'll get it. It's probably one of the kids.'

I dash past her and start down the steps. Rosemary is just behind me. I'm counting rings. It's the fifth ring I've heard when I pick up the phone. I sit down at a chair beside the table near to the desk. Rosemary hovers over me.

I hear the little 'dink' of a long distance call but then nothing, except somebody breathing heavily into the phone.

'Hello, who is this?'

I hear a thick rumbling clearing of a throat, the sound of a sob. Even from this, I recognize Jo Lancaster, my best friend.

'Jo, is that you?'

'I love you.'

Then more hard sobbing. I can't respond. I'm sobbing myself. I hand the phone to Rosemary.

'Jo, is that you?'

There's a long pause, then Rosemary walks over slowly to the table and puts the phone in its cradle.

'He just said he was sorry and hung up.'

We look at each other and break down again. I hold her in my arms. She buries her head into my chin. I can feel her silken skin under her light, white night-gown. Even now, I have my same old trouble. Her hair is tickling my nose. I rub it off in her hair, knowing she'll know, and not caring. After almost forty years, she knows these things about me.

Finally, we push each other away.

'Rosemary, it's starting to get light out. I think you ought to take a shower. Who knows when we'll have a shower again.'

Without a word she starts up the steps, then turns back.

'Would you wake up Will? You know how hard it is for him to get moving in the morning. Make sure he's out of bed. I know he slept because I could hear him snoring last night.'

She goes up the rest of the steps. I turn on the light in the living-room so when the limo comes he'll know we're here and awake. Then I realize I'm stark naked and if any fool is up at this time, by Ocean Grove standards, I'm 'exposing'. I hurry up the stairs.

I wake Will and wait until I'm sure he's up and out of bed. I know better than to carry on a conversation with him. He's a slow starter but his heart's in the right place.

'I know, Dad. I'm up, honest I'm up.'

I go into the bedroom and dress myself in the clothes I laid out last night.

We're ready and on the porch when the limo arrives. We haven't packed much, so Will and I can get everything into the back. It's a real limo with a dark blue plush interior. Will sits in front with the driver because he has such long legs, Rosemary and I sit in back. The driver is good and we feel confident. I'm reminded of a funeral. I've rarely driven in a limo except in those few family funerals I've attended.

The flight is long and boring. I'm torn between mourning and fatigue. Rosemary falls asleep until we reach Chicago and need to change planes. Will drops off to sleep immediately. I try not watching the film.

Chicago to Portland is even longer. Will drops right off again but Rosemary is just staring at the ceiling of the plane with tears running down her face. I don't feel I can interrupt her thinking. I know she's with Kate. I only intrude when the food arrives. I eat, I can always eat. Usually Rosemary can, too, but this time she just plays with the food, pushing most of it aside.

But she drinks a cup of tea.

At Portland, Steve, Bill's younger brother, and Wills are waiting for us at luggage retrieval. We give big hugs to Wills and try not crying too much. Our Will holds his ground, he never hugs anybody, hasn't since he was ten years old.

Steve is tall and thin, even more so than Will. His eyes are red and we hug and shake hands. We're all trying hard to hold it in. He goes to his car and brings it right to the kerb. We throw the baggage in the back and climb in. Will is in front with Steve, and Wills is in back with us. Rosemary is hunting for a third seat belt but there isn't any, so she straps Wills and herself under one.

Steve works himself out of the airport confusion and up on to the highway. He tells us it's the same highway, I-5, on which Kate, Bill, Dayiel and Mia were killed, only they were going the other way, north.

The traffic is horrendous. Steve drives carefully and stays to the right but it seems that every vehicle is towing something, a boat, a trailer, a house trailer or it's a big RV or a huge pick-up with gigantic tyres. I've never been on a highway like this, not even in Los Angeles, and they drive like kids playing bumper cars, constantly cutting in and out, ducking between the gigantic trucks and semi-trailers, steaming along at over seventy miles an hour.

I thought after what had happened to us in the past twenty-four hours I'd never be scared to die again, but I am. I look over at Rosemary. She's white and white knuckled. We turn our attention to Wills, who's been rattling away about some horses they have at the Rodewalds and how this is 'neat' or that is 'neat'. I begin to wonder if anyone's told him what's happened, or is he just so childish he can't comprehend. Then he puts his head on Rosemary's chest and in a choked voice says: 'It was their nap time, Dayiel and Mia. They were probably asleep weren't they. They just didn't wake up.'

Rosemary looks over at me and we're both breathing deeply. She leans her head down so her face is in his hair.

'That's right, Wills. They just went to sleep and never knew what happened. It's terrible that they're gone but I don't think they felt a thing.'

Steve turns off the I-5 and we're on small roads. The unkempt sides of the roads, the house trailers instead of houses, the houses that aren't kept up, make me think of the pine barrens of New Jersey. But it's green. Wills is asleep against Rosemary. He's got to be beat. He's been inside this thing since the beginning.

I begin to dread arriving at a house where I've never been, meeting on such intimate terms people I hardly know. It's *worse* than a wedding.

We twist around a few dirt roads and then pull up in front of a rambling house newly painted, a sort of dark earth pink. There's the most godawful looking tree in the front yard. It looks like something drawn by a talented yet autistic child, too regular and not like a tree at all. It looks like something on which you'd hang your hat.

Betty Rodewald comes down from the front door and off a front porch to meet us. Rosemary unhooks the seat belt and Wills runs to meet her.

She pulls him to her as he's babbling away.

'See, they came. I told you they would. These are Mom's Mom and Dad. They'd be sure to come.'

During the next few hours, as people keep coming with more food, country style, we learn more about what happened. They show us the newspapers. The past two days it's been the headline event in the two Oregon newspapers. The faded, poor-quality colour pictures are gruesome. I can't put it together with our family. It's unreal.

The big question, after the sensationalism of the accident itself, is field burning and why it continues. A farmer named Paul Stutzman started the fire with what he thought was the approval of the DEQ, that is the Department of Environmental Quality, who were keeping surveillance on the valley in helicopters and light planes. Mr Stutzman won't speak to anyone and his son tells the reporters to go away. It all seems so hopeless. I don't really see what can be done. These people obviously don't have the same regard for the environment and human life that we do.

The identification of Bill was made from his dental X-rays. Kate's followed soon after. There was no other way to identify the bodies, they were so badly burned. We really should have stayed in Ocean Grove, spent the day at the beach in an isolated spot and just talked to each other. We shouldn't know this.

It turns out they've arranged with the mortician in the next town, named Dallas, to have the bodies cremated. Betty is Catholic but somewhere along the line, without my noticing, the Catholic church has let up on the temple of the Holy Ghost thing. For other reasons I'd rather they not be cremated but it turns out to be a bit late to stop this. My only insistence is that they not be cremated separately, as planned, but together. After a phone call to Dallas, this is confirmed.

There is pressure on me, as a writer, to come up with something appropriate to have put on the flyer (or whatever it is) that will be distributed at the funeral ceremony. But I have no trouble. They hand me a pencil and paper. I haven't thought about it at all. It flows out of the end of my pencil. It isn't even the kind of thing I'd usually write. I'm more of a mystical poet. I write:

> *They came together*
> *Lived together*
> *Became together*
> *Left together.*

Everybody seems satisfied with this. Then they want me to design a monument. Again I know in my mind, as if I'm being told, exactly what it should be. It's like magic writing.

I take pieces of paper and design a slant-topped sundial with each of their names at each of the cardinal points. Around the sides I write the above poem. At least I have something to do. I want to carve a model of it in wax for the monument maker. We gather all the sealing-wax they use for preserves, I put it in a Number 10 can and melt it. When it's hard, I pound it on the bottom and knock it out. I figure I'll work some more on it in the morning.

We start getting telegrams and telephone calls from our

107

friends all over the world. Several friends of ours and Kate's in Paris and in Munich are actually flying in for the funeral. Camille, Sam and Matt phone from Boston or somewhere to say they're on their way. So much for the fourth commandment.

Betty's in a dither. As I suspected, there's no hotel within twenty miles. There's no space at Steve's apartment with his girl-friend there. Jim, Bill's younger brother, has space for horses but not for people. We start pulling out quilts, blankets, sheets, sleeping bags, blow-up mats, everything we can find. It's going to be a camping funeral. Some people will have to sleep on the lawn. It turns out that we, as sort of the guests of honour, are going to sleep in Bill's room. It's the room he had all the time he lived at home and where he and Kate spent their last night. The cribs are still up in the room. Betty volunteers to take them down but we say it'll be OK. We're so frazzled, not tired, just frazzled, nerves on edge, we can sleep anywhere, that is if we can sleep at all.

We go to bed early. Each of us, I know, is trying not to think about or mention the fact that the sheets we're sleeping on, the blankets we're under, were last slept on and under by Bill and Kate. But we can't help ourselves.

We grab hold of each other and can't stop crying. It's the whole compilation of things, the actual knowing of how they died, how horrible it was, the discussion of the cremation, the formalities. And we're absolutely dead tired. Rosemary's little snooze on the plane and mine in our bed in Ocean Grove last night wasn't enough to support us.

It must be hours that we just cry, very little talk, there isn't much to talk about. How can one have a discussion? Finally, sometime after midnight, Rosemary drops off; I can hear by her regular breathing, sometimes interrupted by a pitiful mewing sound or a sob. But she's asleep. I very carefully untangle myself and stretch out on the bed beside her, on top of the covers.

I must have gone to sleep rather quickly because I have no memory of a long waiting for sleep. This one would be real sleep without chemical assistance. I'm gone.

Sometime before morning I wake. I don't need to go to the bathroom, I just wake naturally. I'm surprised by my inner calm. I know what has happened but it's somehow all inside me, integrated, accepted, in some astonishing way. I lie awake in the dark, in this strange, yet not quite strange bed, the slight fragrance of Kate's perfume, Magie Noire, in the bed sheet. I feel enormously comforted and comfortable. I begin to think I might be having some kind of psychotic experience. It isn't natural to feel so absolutely absolved, or separate, in such a circumstance. I fall back to sleep.

I wake in the morning still in a state of unbelievable calm. I even entertain the idea I might have died in the night and this might be what death is, a totally involving peace.

I turn my head slowly, just enough to see that Rosemary is still asleep. I have no desire whatsoever to move. I stay like that, in some form of suspended animation, for an undefined length of time, watching the sun pass across the low window beside the bed.

Then, the concerns of what must be done this day invade my inner quiet. I carefully slide to the side of the bed, rise to a sitting position. I stay there for several minutes looking out of the window.

Then I stand up. Immediately it is as if I am struck hard from behind. I fall to my knees. Strangely enough, my hands are in fists on the worn shag rug. It's as if I've been knocked down in a football game, clipped, and I can't get my breath for several seconds. Then I can, and begin to sob with such violence I almost throw up. I fight for breath between sobs, but that is only the outside.

Inside I am knowing things I have no way of knowing. My head is spinning. I am on the verge of fainting. I feel Rosemary behind me, hovering over me, her hands on my shaking shoulders. I feel her rolling tears on my bare back.

'What is it dear?! Are you all right? Should I get someone?'

I have just enough contact, strength, to shake my head, no. I stay like that on my knees, not able to stand. Rosemary eases herself on to the rug beside me, her arm over my shoulder, her hand on my quivering wrist. It's as if we're in the starting position of the second period in a college wrestling match. The image, the memory passes through my head, but it is smothered by other images seemingly engraved in my mind, the way nothing I've ever experienced in my life has ever been imprinted.

I try taking deep breaths. Slowly, the shaking comes under control. Rosemary is asking if I think I'm having a stroke or a heart attack, should she call a doctor. I have to tell her something. My first impulse is to try passing off the entire experience, blame it on my hysterical state, keep it to myself. But, almost immediately, I know I can't do this. What I know, or think I know, must be shared, especially with Rosemary. In a certain peculiar way, I'm a messenger.

'Dearest, I've had something happen to me and I don't know how to tell you and still maintain your respect. But I know I must tell you. It is meant that I tell you, even if you can't accept it.'

I settle back to a sitting position on the floor, squatting, between my legs. I'm suddenly aware of my nakedness. I'm in the sunlight coming through the window and I'm naked.

'Rosemary, would you lock the bedroom door? I didn't lock it last night in case we might be needed.'

She pushes herself up, crosses the room, turns the old-fashioned key in the lock. She comes back, folds her legs under her and sits facing me in a modified yoga position. She looks in my eyes, waiting.

'It started, or happened in the middle of the night. We'd both, happily, finally gone to sleep. I woke with this unreal sense of calm, or clarity. It was something like the feeling you have after you've had a long fever and suddenly it's gone. The world seems new and you're an intrinsic part of it. It was something like that. I remember being frightened for my sanity. How could I feel like this when we'd just lost Kate, Bill, Dayiel and Mia. It didn't make sense. Also, it didn't really seem to matter to me that I'd arrived at this strange psychic distance. I don't think it was five minutes before I fell into a deep restorative sleep.

'Rosemary, I woke this morning, refreshed. I didn't want to move, do anything but stay in this nirvana of peace. I still didn't have any idea of why I was so content, soothed; but I knew there were a hundred different things we had to do today and they must be waiting for us downstairs. I eased myself out of bed and stood up. This is where it gets hard to believe, don't interrupt, just listen, please. I want to get it all straight and right.'

I'm trying to sound calm but inside I'm shaking as I come to this part.

'When I stood, it was as if I were knocked down by some powerful force from behind. I found myself hardly breathing, as you found me, when you woke up. But, more than that, I knew all in a flash what had happened to me in the night, what had calmed me, made me feel deeply comforted, despite everything. It all made some kind of sense.'

I take another deep breath, trying to convert something in my mind that wasn't words, into something Rosemary could understand as words, even though I knew she could never know or believe this. Still, I had to tell her. It was part of the entire experience, telling her.

'I was sitting in one of our low beach-chairs on the beach in Ocean Grove with my back to the land, the sun setting over the town behind me. You know how much I like that, the long shadows, the shadows from the ridges in the sand, the changing colour of the water, of the sky, matching the colours almost as complements to the sunset. Then there are the sounds of water at its calmest, rising and falling back on pebbles rolling at the edge of land and sea. It is the most relaxing thing I know of, a natural meditation without effort. It has always been magic.

'Then I see the long shadows of people coming up behind me. I'm disappointed. This is for me a quiet time, not a social event. But it's Kate and Dayiel going past me to the edge of the water. Kate doesn't look over at me. I'm surprised, because she's supposed to be helping you get dinner ready, but I'm even more surprised to see her on the beach. At first, I think it's because she's mad at Bill, and it turns out this is part of it. Then I remember, you know how she is about sand. She never could stand having sand between her toes. So, what's she doing at the beach, walking barefoot?

'Next, Bill comes up on my left side. Kate and Dayiel have passed on my right. He's wearing bathing trunks and one of his

111

loud Hawaiian shirts. He's carrying Mia, the way he does, as if she's a football, in the crook of his huge arm, and hanging over his forearm. He settles in the sand beside me, putting one leg out, his football knee, and he drapes Mia over it. She's wearing a diaper, also some kind of lightweight white shirt and a sunbonnet with ruffles around her face. She's watching my eyes in a way she never has, not as if she's curious about my eyes, but about me. Bill has started making marks in the sand in front of her, the sand collapsing completely, totally, without trace each time. He looks up at me. He has a quizzical smile on his face. He, too, stares into my eyes a long time, in a way he never has. I'm beginning to have a terrible feeling in the pit of my stomach that something horrible has happened. It has, but I have no idea, then. Bill starts that slow shaking of his head which is a sign for me he can't comprehend or believe something.

'"You know, Bert, you're not here and I'm not either. You're in my bed in Falls City, in my bedroom, and I'm still not sure where we are. It seems right now we can be almost anywhere we want. We're hoping to find out more about all this soon. It's really weird."

'He stops. I don't know what he's talking about. It's so far from what I'm seeing, or think I'm seeing, feeling, or think I'm feeling, know, or think I'm knowing, that it's total nonsense to me, like some kind of crazy party game. I just stare at him.

'"Bert, being dead is a hell of a lot different than you might think it is. I'm still not sure what's going on, and I know I'm not supposed to be talking to you, but I wanted you to know. You deserve it. Kate's mad at me for telling you like this, sort of in your dream, but everything was perfect, the place, the time, how it happened to us so fast before we could even think. It all came together and I couldn't resist. There's not much of what we always called time, so I'll hurry.

'"You see, we didn't leave you, *you* left us. It's as if we were all on a giant train or something like that and then we stepped off while you and everybody else just kept on going. That isn't quite right either, but it's close as I can get. I've always been better at numbers than words.

'"But I want you to know we're fine, that we're still

together. There's no way to know what's next but we're not worried about it. That's the important thing. So don't you worry either."

'He looks over, takes his eyes from mine. Kate's coming up the beach with Dayiel dancing around her. She's not coming towards us, she's going to pass right by us again without looking.

'"Kate says I don't know how to let go. But would you do me this one favour. Would you get hold of those bodies that used to be us and take good pictures of them. It's important. It might help stop this damned field burning. It's the field burning more than anything else, that killed us. You'll learn more about it in the next few days. Talk to Steve, tell him about this, he'll help you, I know."

'He pushes himself up. Mia is still watching my eyes. He passes on behind me with her and joins Kate. I can watch their shadows, long and violet-coloured in the sand. I don't turn around. Just as the last shadow is gone I hear Kate's voice.

'"Goodbye Dad, we're sorry."

'Then I turn around and they're gone. The beach is empty. I turn and watch the sea some more.

'Then I must have wakened that first time, when I was so calm. I know now. I really know and I still know.'

I stop. Rosemary is crying, tears just running down her cheeks. She looks me deeply in the eyes.

'That's the most beautiful dream I've ever heard, Bert. Even I, who didn't dream it, feel much more calmly acceptant. I know I can live with it now. I won't say I believe this really happened because I'm not that way. But I believe you believe it happened and that's what's important. I think that's why Bill could come to you, because you could believe. Kate and I never believed this kind of thing. What are you going to do now?'

'I think that's why I've been crying so hard just now. A dream like that should never make anyone cry. But I dread taking those photographs. I can't bear the idea of seeing them like that, burned. I want to remember them the way they were with us that week, or the way they all were in the 'dream'. I don't think I can hire anyone to take those pictures, even if I could find somebody who would. It might even be illegal. I'll have to find someone to give me a hand. Bill suggested Steve. I'll try him first.'

I help Rosemary up off the floor and we make the bed together. I feel so close to her. I wonder what people are going to think when I go downstairs and seem so happy, so full of life instead of death.

After Rosemary washes up, I go in and shower. When I go downstairs, there's all kinds of breakfast fixings and it's serve yourself. I have my blood sugar automatic test kit with me and I need to test before I eat. I go out on to the front porch. Steve comes out behind me. He has his kit, too. It's a remarkable coincidence. We're pricking, making the blood blob, counting, wiping, waiting, while we talk.

'Steve I don't know how to bring this up, but last night I had an amazing experience.'

Then I tell it all as I told it to Rosemary. Steve looks at me in the strong morning light.

'That's Bill, all right. He fought field burning tooth and nail. He could never let go, even if he was dead. You should have seen him play football or basketball. Never-say-die-Rodewald we called him.'

'The main thing is, can you help me, Steve? Bill sort of said you would. I need to see those bodies and take pictures of them. I dread the whole thing, but I feel it's some kind of a mandate from Bill.'

'I can call John, the mortician in Dallas, and take you there. I have a camera, too. But let's eat first.'

'I'd like to try keeping this to ourselves, Steve. It sounds so crazy, I don't want to try explaining to anybody else.'

'I'll call from the upstairs phone.'

We have a great breakfast. There are pans after pans of good scrambled eggs. Each of us washes out his or her dishes in a huge kitchen sink. I've just finished mine when I catch Steve at the front door signalling me. I go over.

'John says the bodies are at the coroner's but he'll get them to the mortuary if we want. He says they're pretty awful and he doesn't recommend our looking at them.'

'What'd you tell him?'

'I didn't tell him anything, but I made arrangements for us to be there at one o'clock. Is that OK?'

'Thanks, Steve. I'll work on the model for the monument while we're waiting.'

'Dad had all the tools you'll ever need. They're out in the back shed. But you don't have to do this right now. It can wait.'

'I want to. I'll be better off out there working with your dad's tools than inside with everybody. I need time to be alone; this will be my excuse.'

Steve takes me out to a really great workshop, all in wood, with nails driven into the walls for hanging tools and each tool marked in outline against the wall, so anybody can know where each tool goes and his dad could know if a tool were missing. With three boys, I'm sure he had to keep track of his tools.

Steve brings out the Number 10 can with the wax mould in it and some knives. He clears the work table, putting tools back in place.

'This should be just the kind of place for you. I can't tell you how much we all appreciate your doing this, especially now, considering all that's happened.'

He goes right out. I wonder if he thinks I would be making this model for a monument if practically our whole family hadn't been killed. I'm sure he's as upset as I am.

I spend the entire morning carving away until the monument in my mind begins to appear. Around the sides I carve in the words of the poem. I find an old four penny nail and use it for the gnomon. I set it at an angle equal to the angle of the sundial face. For the cardinal points, I carve in Bill at north or twelve o'clock, Kate at south or six o'clock, and Mia on one side, at nine o'clock, that is, west, and Dayiel at three o'clock, or east. I find some gold paint in the paint closet, and with a small brush fill in the indentations of the carving.

It doesn't look funereal at all and it certainly makes me feel much better, as if I've done *something*, at least. Throughout the whole job, I can feel Bill hovering near but I hear or see nothing. It is only my imagination.

Sometimes one person or another will drift in but I don't

look up. It doesn't happen too often, so I imagine Steve has given the word. Rosemary comes briefly to sit by and watch quietly. I look up at her, and we smile but don't say anything. I think it's as hard for her to speak as it is for me. She puts her hand on my shoulder as she leaves. I continue working, turning the model in different directions to see how it reacts to the lighting until it feels right. Steve comes in. He's enthusiastic about the monument-sundial model.

'First we should eat, then take off for Dallas. John phoned and said he managed to get the bodies from the coroner's office but they aren't happy about it.'

'Well, I assure you, Steve, it's something that has to be done. It won't be much of a pleasure, but sometimes things just have to be done. I have my camera with me, but I don't have much film. Is there a place in Dallas where we can buy film?'

'Sure, and I'll bring my camera too. We can buy any film we'll need. The same place does really good work on developing, and they're pretty fast if we make it a rush order.'

'Good, I'll clean this up and come in soon. What's the chance we can go to some place where they cut marble and granite?'

'In Salem, there's a place called Capitol Monuments. They cut the little plaque for Dad's grave. We can stop in there after we go to John's. In fact, we can do that while we're waiting for the film to be developed. Everything will be closed tomorrow, Sunday.'

'That's what we'll do then. I'll be inside in a minute or two.'

Inside there's a mob scene. Everyone is so nervous and so glad to see each other it's more like a wedding than a funeral. I say hello to everybody, trying not to act too much the hypocrite, but not wanting to offend their sensibilities. I'm just not totally broken up the way I was before. Rosemary's in good form, too. These people must think we're the most cold-hearted parents and grandparents in the world. Camille is making up for us. She and Sam also arrived this morning. She's crying up a storm. Those babies were practically like her own; she often took care of them. She and Kate were beginning to be really close, too, even though they had entirely different personalities. Her entire face is swollen and wet all over as if she's been running.

It's a quarter past twelve and I eat hurriedly. I'm not really hungry but I don't want to feel sick or weak, especially now. Steve gives me the eye and goes out of the front door. I wait about two minutes, then follow him. He has his car parked outside the gate and the motor's running. I dash into the workshop and pick up the model; I've stashed my camera in the workshop because I've been taking photos of the model as it's come along. I mount the model on a small piece of plywood. I climb into the front seat beside Steve.

The trip to Dallas is quick and we don't talk much. We stop first at the photo shop and buy three rolls of film, thirty-five millimetre, colour, print, twenty-four exposures. We figure that should do. Then we drive to the mortuary. It isn't as ugly as I thought it would be. In fact it's quite handsome, natural woods and tinted glass. It's also bigger than I'd expected.

But when we go in, it's a mortuary all right. There are the smells and also the quiet. A sandy-haired, slightly balding man comes out from a small office to greet us. Steve shakes hands with him and introduces us. John, the mortician, looks at me quizzically.

'Are you sure you want to do this? I don't recommend it.'

I nod. I don't want to talk too much. I'm on the edge of what I can handle. Being in the mortuary where my family is being stored is getting to me.

'Have you ever seen badly burned human bodies before?'

I nod again, not trusting myself to speak. I must look pretty white or green. He suggests we sit down in some comfortable chairs grouped in a semicircle in a small ante-room. We sit. I feel I should say something but I don't want to tell him about Bill's visit to me. I'm sure morticians hear more crazy stories than they really want to. I try answering his question.

'I was in World War Two and helped pull bodies out of tanks after they'd burned, both American and German. I have a good idea of what it's like. Mostly I remember the smell.'

'Well, this will be different. This is your family, not complete strangers. I've sprinkled formaldehyde over the bodies to keep down the smell and to slow down the natural decomposition that would occur. Because we've had to hold the bodies for so long, we've also had to keep them in a cold locker. That's one of the reasons they were at the coroner's; I don't have enough cold storage space for them.'

'I understand.'

I understand, but I'm beginning to want to back out of the whole thing. I can see by Steve's colour he's having some of the same feelings. I check my camera and stand up. Steve stands, too. John gets up with us. He leads the way down a narrow corridor to the back of the building. There's a door at the end of the corridor. I guess that's the entrance through which they bring the bodies to cause a minimum of disturbance for the neighbours.

We walk into the last door on the right. There's the smell all right but it's covered partly by a chemical smell. It reminds me of biology class at UCLA. There are four tables, a small one just where we came in, then another small one, then two larger tables deeper in the room. There are high windows over the tables. Each table is covered with a waterproof cover, black on one side and yellow on the other. John steps ahead of us. He takes hold of the cover on the first small table and turns to us.

'This is going to be difficult for you. If you feel it is too much, give me a signal. I'll cover the body and we'll get out of here.'

He pauses, watching us.

'This one is the one who burned the least, the little baby, Mia.'

Steve and I back off a little and he slowly, gently, removes the cover. My first reaction is that she looks exactly like the bodies which were dug up at Pompeii and Herculaneum. She's all white and her features are obliterated but it is definitely the form of a little girl. Her left foot has been broken off just above the ankle but is still hanging by a piece of what was once flesh. In places, we can see the charred sections of her body which were not covered by the formaldehyde powder.

Steve and I look at each other. We're both sighing and taking deep breaths. John is watching us carefully.

'Do you want me to cover her again?'

I figure I can make it. I look at Steve. He nods. I think he nods that we should go on, but I'm not sure. My hands are shaking. I manage to make the settings for my camera, then focus on the baby. I know I'm crying. This is far from every memory I have of Mia. It's hard to keep it together. I take shots from the side, then from on top, leaning over, smelling the cloying yet sharp odour, the combination of the chemical and decomposition. Steve is doing the same thing. John covers Mia and leads us out into the corridor.

'Look, I don't know why you two are doing this but I don't want to have any more dead bodies around here. I think you're pushing yourselves beyond what you can handle. I'm a professional, but I don't think I could take pictures like that of my family if something terrible like this happened.'

Steve and I are leaning back against the wall of the corridor, breathing deeply, trying to recover. I could easily up-chuck if I let myself.

'We're OK. It's just hard. We really want to have these pictures, the last part of some of the most lovely people in the world. OK, Steve? Shall we go back?'

He nods his head. John opens the door again. The smell this time isn't so bad. It's in our clothes now, so the shock isn't as great. John goes to the other small table. He pulls off the cloth. This time it's much harder. Somehow, in the accident, Dayiel lost the top of her skull. The striations of her brain are visible. She's also lost her arms, from the tops above the elbows down, and her legs from above the knees. If she were alive, she'd be a 'basket-case baby', like those thalidomide cases in Germany. I can't believe this is the beautiful Dayiel, a child who never stopped, with deep blue eyes, a lively expression and golden hair. There is a clump of darkened hair at her neck that I think could be her hair.

I start photographing and feel the room beginning to spin around. I grab hold of the table edge Dayiel's on. John moves towards me, but I'm better. I lean over to take a photo from above. I hear Steve. He's leaned against the wall behind us and is slowly sliding down. John grabs him by the arm and takes him out. I stay on and take a few more photos of Dayiel, knowing it isn't really her, impressed by how we are all so fooled by the physical, into thinking that this is what we *are*. What must it be for her having to change everything, be in another world when she is so young. But then the whole idea of age is only one part of our limitations. It only deals with how long we've been in a particular body, or some such thing.

Thinking these thoughts comforts me. So I regain my equilibrium. I go out to the corridor. Steve and John have gone up to the ante-chamber again and are sitting down. I join them. John turns towards me.

'Steve says he's ready to go back. He wants to see his brother for the last time. I'm not so sure it's a good idea.'

I look at John and then at Steve.

'Don't come back, Steve, if it's too much. I know your family is Catholic. I don't know how much of it you believe; but if you accept the idea of the spirit, then you know that what we're looking at in there is only the empty body they left behind. I know it's horrible from a human point of view but it just isn't them any more.'

Steve has leaned over and is looking at his hands, fooling with his camera. His colour is coming back. He looks up at me.

'OK, you're right. I'm ready. I have a feeling this is what Bill meant and this is a kind of test or something. Let's go.'

We walk down the corridor again, John leading the way. I check to see how much film I have left on the roll; enough for two pictures, then I'll need to change rolls. I have a roll in my pocket.

We go into the room. I try not to breathe deeply. John lifts the cover off one of the larger tables. It takes my breath away. It's Bill! He has his head arched back so I can see under his neck. This time it's like that wonderful statue in Amsterdam by Zadko. The stumps of both his arms are thrown up over his head as if he's reaching for the sky. His mouth is open as in a scream. It's a dreadful sight as a reality. Steve just stares. I look into his face. He's smiling a mirthless smile.

'It's exactly the way he'd go, screaming, reaching for a way out. I'm glad I've seen this. It helps me accept things. Bill was my big brother. He never gave up. Part of this whole horror for me has been that he didn't do anything. I can see now he was trying the best he could. He was "never say die" Rodewald, right up to the end.'

We start photographing. Even burned down to the bones as he is, it's obvious he was a big and powerful man. His legs are shattered in pieces, not more than three inches each. His arms are above his head but his shoulders have been driven right out of the sockets. In his open, screaming mouth all his teeth are visible like a skull, the skin of the face burned away.

I note all this as I take the first two photos, then change film. Mine is an old-fashioned camera with no automatic rewind and load. I rewind by hand, then engage the spool with shaking hands, close the cover, cock it a few times and start taking pictures. Steve is finished with his and stands looking at his brother. He's crying.

I ask if we can take a little break before I look at Kate. I know this is going to be the hardest for me. All the games we played together, the thousands of books I've read to her, the nights up with her when she was sick, the fun pushing her on a swing or around on a playground carousel, or sometimes on a real carousel, trying to grab rings and never getting any, and she'd laugh. There's so much binding people together it's hard to let go.

We go back in. John pulls the cover down towards her feet. The yellow and black plastic reminds me of so many auto accidents I've seen or helped with in my more than fifty years on the road. I never thought I'd see our first born wrapped up in one.

She's the least recognizable. The lower part of her trunk is a mass of unburned but seared intestines, other organs. Here, she seems the least burned. But her legs, her wonderful long legs are broken into pieces like a jigsaw puzzle or the bones found in the ground and pieced together to make a dinosaur. When I look at her face, calm, the mouth closed, her beautiful green eyes, now only holes in blackened bone, I almost can't make it. I keep trying to keep my eye to the viewfinder of my camera. It's more as if I'm seeing it on television or something else artificial not real.

I can't take any more. I go out of the door into the hall. Steve follows me. John covers Kate, then comes out too. Steve and I are soaking wet from sweat. My knees feel weak. The sweat on my forehead is cold. John leads us down to the couches and comes back in a few minutes with a shot of whisky for each of us. I sip mine, Steve downs his like a true Oregonian. John stands in front of us.

'Well, I didn't think you'd make it. That was bad. I want you both to know how sorry I am this had to happen. There's no excuse for a civilized state like Oregon to have field burning still going on. These four young people aren't the first field burning victims I've buried from around here. It's a disgrace.'

We take the film out of our cameras. John goes back into his office. By the time I finish rolling the film out of my camera I feel somewhat better. At least I'm not sweating. I head for the rest-room. It is such a hot, sweaty day I want to freshen up. I find the rest-room in the corridor leading away from the one where we saw the bodies.

I take off my shirt and undershirt. They are soaking wet. I'm a big sweater. I fill the little basin with water and dunk both shirt and undershirt into it. I push down and slosh them around to get the nervous smell out. I can't be any wetter. Then I wring them out as best I can and slide them back on. It is refreshing. Steve comes into the rest-room. I tell him what I've done. He's only wearing a T-shirt. He pulls it over his head and does the same thing. He is thin, with strong arms and more hairy than I thought he'd be but not as hairy as Bill.

'What a great idea. I smell like a horse with scurvy.' He uses his wet T-shirt to wipe under his arms and down his stomach, then rinses it again before he wrings it out and slides it back on. We leave the rest-room refreshed and ready for the Oregon heat.

The film place is nearby. We ask to have only the negatives made. We'll choose which ones to have printed. It seems they can do it all in one day.

We head for Salem, the capital of the state of Oregon. I'm wondering if the monument place is CAPITOL MONUMENTS or CAPITAL MONUMENTS. Most Americans don't know or pronounce the difference. The *capitol* building has to be here in Salem, but Salem is the *capital* city of Oregon.

It turns out to be CAPITOL MONUMENTS. They're open. I take the model out of the car. Steve begins talking to a round-faced man. They're surrounded by all kinds of monuments and slabs of marble. It's like an indoor cemetery. Steve is saying he's the brother of Bill Rodewald who was killed in the I-5 crash. He introduces me and the man is very sympathetic. I guess tombstone builders have to learn sympathy as much as morticians.

I show him the model and explain what I want. He has trouble catching on to the idea that I'm not as concerned about its being a functioning sundial as I am that it be a symbol of everlasting life, the constant revolving of the sun.

We talk about the kind of stone. There must be fifty different kinds to choose from. I want one which is a rich, warm grey but he tells me it won't weather the way another granite called Sierra would. There's not much difference so I agree to the Sierra. He doesn't have any in stock but he can order it. That's OK with me. There's no way I can stay to see it finished. I'm hoping I'll never come back to Oregon again in my life. I'll most likely never see it.

The CAPITOL man, whose name I forget, begins making drawings to approximate my model. He must have flunked industrial drawing in high school. I keep correcting his perspective and isometric projections. Steve and I decide to have the two family names carved on the front of the monument. Under it, the brief poem. The cardinal points, as on my model, would be carved as well. We tell him we want the colour in the engraving to be black, not gold as in my model. He tells us he'll mail a full-sized styrofoam mock-up to me in New Jersey. I give him my address. He says the monument in the cemetery will come to about five thousand dollars. I tell him I'll pay after I've seen the mock-up and made corrections.

Steve looks at his watch. We get out of the graveyard of polished stones and into the heat again. We drive back to the film place. Steve has air-conditioning, but even so, it's hot. We get to the film store just as it's re-opening. I realize we haven't had anything to eat.

We're shocked when we look at the negatives. Practically none of them are usable. We were so nervous and shaken we seem to have made every mistake possible. It's three o'clock. The next day is Sunday and then there's the funeral. We ask how soon they'd need new negatives in order to have them ready by Monday. They close at six. Steve uses their phone and phones the mortuary. John says he hasn't sent the bodies back but can't hold them past four because the coroner's office closes at five on Saturdays.

We buy more film. We drive like madmen to the mortuary. We're out and in the back room in five minutes. John shows us some Polaroid shots his son has taken. They'll probably be good enough if we don't do it right this time.

We're much more calm and collected this time. I check every move, every setting on my camera to get it right. It's astounding how the human mind can adjust to almost anything. We get the photos shot in half an hour. We're both crying as we go along but we're functioning. We thank John profusely. Nobody could be nicer under such conditions.

We get the film out of the camera and delivered to the photo shop in plenty of time. Steve takes his camera from me. I was unloading as he was driving. They tell us we can see the negatives and maybe positive direct prints before they close, if we want to wait. I think they've looked at the work we did before and know what we're doing. They're very considerate. Two young women run the place. We say we'll be back at ten minutes to six. We walk out into the heat again. Nobody should have to die in weather like this. Steve turns away from his car.

'I need a beer. I know a good, dark, air-conditioned place about half a block from here.'

'Sounds good to me, Steve. I'm starving and I'll go any place that's cool.'

We go into the back of a wood-panelled place with the bar up front. Steve orders two draught beers on the way in. I can feel myself fading. I lean back in my chair. Steve quaffs off his beer with only one stop. It's so cold it hurts my eyes.

'Steve, you know what I'd like to do while we're waiting for those photos?'

It's obviously a rhetorical question, but I think Steve's expecting anything from me.

'How far is it from here to where the accident happened? Do you think we could get from here to there and back before the photo shop closes?'

Steve stares at the ceiling, then sucks out the foamy dregs of his beer.

'We could do it, but it'll be close. I don't think we'll find anything anyway. The road is black and the grass is burned there, but they cleared everything away with big equipment. I watched some of it on television.'

'I'd really just like to see the last things they saw. It would bring me closer to them.'

Steve stands up, pushes back his chair.

'OK, let's go then. We have about two hours, that should do it.'

He's out of the door. I take a last slug of beer. I catch up with him. The heat hits us again. The car's still where we left it at the mortuary.

Steve drives faster than before but still not so fast that I'm uncomfortable. We don't talk too much. Steve keeps looking at his watch.

'We'll make it and have about ten minutes to look around if we want. I haven't been here myself, just didn't have the nerve. We'll need to go down about twelve miles past to find an on-ramp to the I-5. There's some kind of construction going on in the southbound lane there. But I think we'll make it.'

We drive on to the I-5 going north and I'm looking out of the windows, wondering just what Kate or Bill or any of the kids might have seen. I'm hoping for some contact from them. I'm so close to where they last were in this world, although four days have passed. The newspapers said the accident seemed to have happened around four o'clock. It's around four, a little after.

But all I experience in the landscape is a weird frozen quality, as if nobody has ever been here. There's a lovely little hill in the generally flat country to my right. Kate must have noticed that. As a geologist, this strange formation would mean

125

something to her.

Both north- and southbound traffic is on the north side with us. The trucks are enormous and are going too fast for the density of traffic. There's no passing. These guys have got to make up time. We open up again, the south traffic back in its own lane, and we see where the accident was. Steve pulls over. We get out in the slanting sun and look. The road bed is cracked from the intense heat of the crash. I only looked briefly at the newspapers everybody kept pushing into my face last night because I wasn't ready. But I remember the fire burned for hours. It seems diesel fuel leaked out of a truck and combined with a truck filled with wood chips, making quite a fire. I find a piece of metal on the road. I shine it up and it's the name plate of a Corvair. We have to be careful because the cars are tearing by, nobody going under seventy.

'Bert, we'd better get going. I don't know if I can take this any longer and that photo shop might close on us. It's hard to predict traffic at this time of night.'

We hop back in the car and head north, continuing the trip that Kate, Bill, Dayiel and Mia never finished.

We arrive at the photo shop before a quarter to six. The girls pull out both the film and prints. They have a back light wall and magnifying glasses for us to look at the negatives and prints. It's almost worse than the reality. This time we did it right. Steve wants me to choose. I'm not sure what Bill wanted except somehow these photos were supposed to help fight the field burning. I try selecting photos which best show the terrible damage done to their bodies. I know that after this, only the photos can ever show that. Two days from now, the rest of the cremation will be done and as far as we mere mortals are concerned, they won't exist any more.

I select twenty of the photos for full-scale enlargement. The rest of the negatives and proofs I put in a separate packet. I'm glad I have a significant amount of cash with me because I forgot my cheque book. I don't want to use plastic. One of the girls, the smaller, not so pretty one, gets up her nerve.

'Are these photos of the victims of the I-5 crash Wednesday?'

'That's right.'

Steve looks at me to see if it's all right to tell them.

'Are you from the police? How did you get these pictures? I couldn't help looking at them. They're terrible!'

We're quiet. She has a right to know.

'No. I'm the father of the woman and grandfather to the two babies. My friend here is the brother to the man. We took these pictures so we'd have something to remember them by.'

She looks to see if I'm kidding, sees I'm not, puts her hand to her mouth.

'But what a terrible way to remember them. I don't know how you could have taken these pictures. Didn't I just say that to you, Diana?'

'Well, we did. In a way, we had to. How much will I owe you for all this work? It's very well done. Would you please write out the bill for the enlargements, and for the development and proofs? I'll pay now. My friend will pick them up when they're ready.'

She takes a form and checks off the negatives to be enlarged, peering at the numbers in the margin. She notes the cost of the development and proofs separately. It comes to just under two hundred dollars. I take two 100 dollar bills out of my pocket. She peers at them, to check if they're real, I think. She gives me the change.

'We're terribly sorry about what happened. Isn't that field burning awful?'

'I don't know, except it killed my family. We don't allow things like this where I live.'

We turn and leave. It's hot in the car. Even at six o'clock in the evening it's hot. But it is August. Steve turns up the air conditioner. I lay my head back on the head-rest. My eyes feel bare. But we did get it done: everything, the monument, the pictures. Maybe I can sleep tonight. I should, I'm dead tired. I dread the funeral. I own one suit, one white shirt, one tie, one decent pair of shoes. Getting dressed up for things is not my style.

Track down the clues to *great travel* with ODYSSEY GUIDES

Crack the case; how anthropologist/ author Françoise Pommaret unlocks the secrets of the red-robed lamas

Dig beneath the surface and unearth a civilization as old as ancient Egypt

Baffled by this inscrutable land? Peek behind the mask and Japan's true identity will be revealed

Decipher the cryptic writing on the wall in this land of medieval watchtowers and cave monasteries

Catch a train; the Himalayas are motive enough for a summer retreat

Be tempted into the Garden of Europe. Discover the mysticism of Portugal's pagan cults.

Plan your escape to the tropical beaches and pristine coral reefs of the Indian Ocean

IT'S A CRIME NOT TO OWN ONE!

Distributed by Hodder & Stoughton Publishers
These and other titles are available at all major book stores

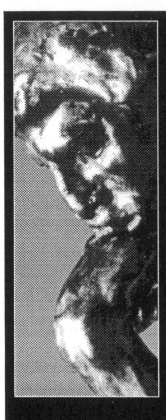

The thinking persons choice...

£1
Out on
Tuesdays

London's Listing Guide

MONA SIMPSON
RAMADAN

'Welcome in Egypt,' a large man said.

Egypt, that first brass afternoon in spring, may have been the most stylish place I ever saw on the earth. Nobody had ever told me about the cars. The cars were old German and American models from the fifties and sixties, black and rounded. They honked and shined everywhere, and I found a driver to Alexandria with my guidebook propped between two pronged fingers like a piece of music. Alexandria was a long way—two guys turned me down before this one. He was handsome and young, with many teeth, and he had a dry grassy smell the closer I stood to him. We bargained a price in dollars. I still had to get pounds. He knew almost no English. He had a book. I sat in the back of the old Mercedes on deep leather seats made soft with time and watched out of the rolled-down windows as we left Cairo in a circle like a maze and drove north into the horizon of cypresses, eucalyptus and olive trees. It was good.

There was so much sky. The ground and trees, people and even buildings rose about an inch and the rest was sky. It was 24 February. I wanted to remember the day. I lay my head back on the seat and the smell of earth rolled over me. This wasn't desert as I'd expected. It was dirt, not light sand; the vegetation was scarce and sombre. Ragged trees moved slightly in the soft wind, and they seemed to whine and creak. Date palm and sycamore. Closer in, there were acacia, juniper, jacaranda and grass.

I felt looser in my clothes when I couldn't see Cairo behind us any more. We were on an old road. The structures you saw in the distance looked small, made of concrete and mud. A rich weedy taste came through the air. I thought of my father and how, even though he was a boy who grew up here in this old slow country, he'd moved in suits and silk ties all over the world. I'd travelled too. I'd driven cross-country, had my college summer in Europe; even my grandmother, in Wisconsin, had been around the world. But do we, any of us, love more?

If this was Egypt, maybe that explained Wisconsin. His existence there. On the road ahead of us I saw a small lake and then a mountain, which disappeared when we came close. I'd been told about mirages in school, when I learned the word,

133

but I'd never seen one. Maybe it took a desert to produce them. Once in a while the driver turned to me and we'd try to talk but it was too hard, so he'd fall back to driving, which he did with an evenness and a happy hum that seemed as odd and discordant as sitar music. He had a vague smile which seemed to move through a sort of plot sequence. I rested back on the seat, thinking how I'd like to sleep with this boy just once, tonight, in my hotel room and wondering if I could, how this worked and whether I should give him money. This was so foreign no one would know. No one ever. For the rest of my life no one would know.

I stared at the back of his neck. His hair was cut short but it still curled. Below the line of hair were two lines of sweat, tiny drops balanced on the dark taut skin. At that moment I thought how hard it was to be a man. The distance between imagining and placing a hand in the world on to someone's skin—I didn't know how that happened. That seemed enormous. Even when there were two cultures and no language and you had the money. But no. That wasn't good. Being bought with money could harm anyone.

I tapped his shoulder—his skin through the cotton was warm—and pointed for him to stop at a market, a bazaar of some kind by the side of the road. It looked like a farm food stand anywhere in America, except the trees were high date palms. I was hungry. He pulled over the Mercedes, its bulk calming smoothly on the dirt gravel pass. We got out. The canvas- and tin-roofed tents shaded jars of oil, dates still on the branch, almonds, pine nuts, diamond-cut pastries in tin pans that ran with honey, hazed by close thick black flies, pomegranates, olives, figs open and red, dusty purple on the outside. A thin man, dark-skinned with almost no hair on his legs and arms and head, sat cross-legged on a striped rug on the uneven ground. His eyes were nearly closed. A clear glass jar, like one you would buy jam in, sat full by his knee. I tried to get close. I browsed by a table with nothing recognizable on it, some kind of cheese in water, I thought. I saw then in his jar: a coiled snake; I couldn't tell dead or alive.

I wanted figs, dates and almonds and started to gather them in a brown paper bag, but my driver came up and with elaborate arm motions pointed to his chest, establishing, I'll do this, without words. The thin man's flat sunken mouth smiled a big smile. He tried to take her and was caught. She's an American, it's all game.

Walking back to the car with my bag of fruit, I heard a familiar monotonous sound. I walked across the sand and looked behind the tent. A rickety ping-pong table was set up on the ground and two dark boys were playing. Then we were driving again, and he conducted a long speech to me in Arabic, probably about how much money he'd saved me, and I murmured something to make it seem I understood. 'Is no good for you, is better for you,' was all I made out from his speech. His one arm sometimes lifted off the wheel, articulate and graceful, but I wished I could settle it back to driving and I ate the fresh dates, the skins crumbling like sugar and the fruit inside melting like honey. I could eat like this for a hundred years. In the back seat there was a long soft breeze and sun on the left side, so I took off my shoes and my long shirt and just lay down in my tank top and skirt, legs bare, feet on the leather, feeling it almost like another skin. I was sort of asleep but not really. The breeze played on my belly, my upper arms, the bones of my neck. It was good. The smell of the fruit on the foot-space swelled up in shells of air.

Before I left, I'd wanted to find some Arabs to write things down for me. I stopped at the place across from the school that sold hummus and tabouli and shish kebab in pita. But the guys there turned out to be Israelis. Nice guys. They gave me a felafel and suggested that I check the university. It would have to have some kind of Arab Studies department.

I asked directions and went upstairs. On a third floor corner, I found Near Eastern Studies. A woman in black jeans and a black turtle-neck stood near a floor-to-ceiling wire cage which held a parrot. Inside the cage, which looked home-made, was a large, driftwood branch where the parrot perched. The woman held a finger to the bird. From the glint of jewel, I saw she was married. She was dark-skinned, wide-eyed, with an extremely full, flower-shaped mouth. She sounded younger than she looked.

'I'm Mayan Atassi.' That was the first time I'd said it since

Ted Stevenson broke our names and then returned to randomness. 'I'm looking for someone Egyptian.'

The parrot flapped its long wings and squawked. She laughed. 'Egyptian. Let's see. Professor Kamal is,' she said, 'but he's on leave in Paris this year.'

'You're not Egyptian?' I said.

'No, I'm from Lebanon,' she said. My whole life I'd heard of Beirut and how it was the Switzerland of the Middle East. I knew that I had been conceived there.

'Do you know Arabic?'

'Yes, mmhmm.'

I began to explain. My mother never wanted me to be alone with my dad. 'He could have you on a plane to Egypt in ten minutes,' she'd snap her fingers, 'and they'd have you married off and swelled up pregnant at fourteen. That's what they do to girls over there. Girls are nothing.'

'What about going to college?' I'd said.

'College, in Egypt?' she said. She burst out with a bitter-rinded laugh. 'Forget it.'

I was grown up now and being pregnant didn't seem only shame. It appeared even beautiful, a common thing. It was strange having outlived the life with my mother: I was forever rediscovering little things that I had believed and assumed and were not true. Anyway, I might never be able to get pregnant and that was because of me. I'd dieted too much when I was in high school.

On three sheets of paper, the woman with the parrot wrote in Arabic the Station Street address, my address in America, and a little paragraph that I dictated saying who I was and that I was looking for my father whom I hadn't seen in years, and his name. I looked at her ring while she wrote. It was dark gold, the diamond capped on either side by bright blue-green gems cut in squares.

I opened my wallet and slipped the three papers in the deepest part. They became treasures. She asked me if I would come back when I returned and tell her what happened.

I was half-way down the hall, a clean echoing hall of black tiles, and then I ran back. 'Do you know what the weather is like there?'

She stepped out from behind the desk. She was a plump-cheeked woman, big breasted, wonderful looking. 'Nice. Perfect. Like your San Francisco.'

S ome time later he made a punctuating noise in the front and I sat up. I saw Alexandria in the distance, like a series of half staircases on a hill. This was the place my father grew up. It was early evening, seven o'clock and not much light. The roads (some of them) looked older than the Ottoman empire but were still used, not kept for antique. There were geraniums in the windows, like Paris. The stone and plaster were crumbling and dirty. A lot of the houses had clay pots on the roofs. I wondered why. Some of the buildings had a white sheen, with mosaic. The streets were quieter than Cairo, the neighbourhoods lower, the old sun like a bucket full of water spilled on the bricks. This was a smaller city, I guessed, and was supposed to be holy. I knew that. Not only for me.

'*Mumkin ahgiz ohda ghur-fa min hi-na?*'

I read to him from the guidebook but he didn't understand. Then I gave up and moved behind his shoulder and showed him where it was printed in Arabic calligraphy, pointing with my finger-nail while the car moved unevenly over the bricks. I wanted a hotel. He put his hand to his forehead, and then exploded in head-nodding. He was so young. His shirt was striped, yellow and green. Just then I noticed a band aid on his right arm, near the elbow, a band aid printed with circus animals, the kind we always wanted as children. Is that what became of circus band aids? The surplus shipped to the Third World?

We turned a corner and beyond us was the Mediterranean, blue and green and moving with unrest, a sea of barking dogs. He drove me to an ugly hotel, modern and run-down. I said no, crossed my arms, and found the word for old in the guidebook. This made him think a moment and then he got it, and the next place was right: white and Persian-looking, with small cracks snaking down the towers. He parked the Mercedes, pulled the keys out and came inside with me, carrying the pack. It seemed too hard to argue. He wanted to deal with the desk for me, so I stood next to him, holding out my credit card. The man behind the desk took it, produced a key and that was the end of it. An old cage elevator, with script I could not read, lyrical cursives strewn in fancy metal painted white, stopped at the ninth floor where the smell of old geraniums came profuse and dusty and breath-stopping almost: I followed and he opened the door of my room and it was good.

French doors opened to a small terrace and the sunset fired outside. I looked in the bathroom: it was completely tiled, even the ceiling. You could wash it out with a hose. The bed was plain and white; a small prayer rug waited in one corner. The carpet was a very faded red, and dirty.

My driver put my backpack down and stood there.

I pulled my wallet out of the pack and paid him the amount we agreed, plus ten dollars.

He counted slowly, with complication, twice, then his face cleared and he handed me back ten one dollar bills.

I shook my head no, pointed—for you—then I grabbed the phrase book and tried to find the words that meant 'for the children.' In the guidebook, it said you were supposed to say 'for the children.' He looked pretty young to have children and I couldn't find the damn phrase anyway, so I pushed the money back into his hand and he shook his head no, and I put my hands behind my back meaning I won't take it and then he pushed my shoulders, gentle but a real push, the money held up in his hand between us, and for a minute we didn't know what was happening and then we were falling back, first me on the bed and then him.

His skin stretched and spread taut wings from his neck to his top chest bones. I remembered that he was young, probably younger than twenty. I wanted to hear his name. I didn't want it to be Atassi. He could have been. My father might have come back. Then I remembered my father telling me around the old kitchen table, 'If I went back, I'd be running the country. I was the John F. Kennedy of Egypt.' Well, he wasn't running the country. I read the newspapers. I knew those people's names. He said so little to us that I saved every sentence. I could lift one up like a bracelet or strand of pearls from a box. As if any young man could be held responsible for grandiose dreams whispered to an infant daughter, when he was new in a country and still thought everything was possible.

But he could have come back. It was more than twenty years ago he'd said that. He was a very young man then.

I rolled over on my belly, reached down for the guidebook. My shoes fell off the side of the bed. He pulled me back by my ankle. I felt his fingers like a bracelet. I rifled through the pages. There it was; My name is ____. 'Ismee Mayan Atassi,' I said.

He pointed to his chest. 'Ramazan el-Said. I was born during the Ramadan, so my mother called me that.'

OK. Fine. I lay back on the bed; the book dropped. This was good. We couldn't say a word and I'd stopped trying, but maybe because of that something else worked. I always talked too much in bed anyway. I lay back and wished he would touch my neck for some reason, I don't know why, and I don't know if I'd ever wanted that or thought that before, my neck, but he did, first with his fingers, hard so I felt my pulse flutter. I didn't know if it would be different or the same so far away with someone not in my language, a complete stranger, but I watched the fan in the ceiling slowly mark the room with carousel shadows and in a minute I was lifting my hips to shrug my skirt off and then we were both naked, he was dark and thin and not different really. I touched him and looked in his face, his cheeks seemed to spread wider apart and questions stood like cool statues in his eyes and I wanted him and started it and then it began. It went on a long time, well into first dark, it never really stopped. I'd turn over on my side and clutch some sheet around me and look out of the windows at the clear stars and he'd be on my back with his hands and mouth and then something would feel like a shot, absolute and four-pointed but blooming pleasure and we'd begin again and it went on so long sometimes I'd forget. I'd feel I was the man, entering him and he seemed that way too, opened, split, eyes shallowing up like hungry fish on the surface, as if in the night we traded who owned the outside and the inside, who could penetrate and who could enclose. The stranger was in me and I wanted that. I finally fell asleep. He woke me and I heard water rushing. It was still dark. I dragged the sheet behind me to the

window, where there was one star that almost hurt to look at, a
too proud diamond, somebody else's, and I wondered why he'd
woken me so late or so early, and then he pushed me to the
bathroom where he'd run a deep tub with a flower floating on the
top. The whole thing smelled almond and he put me in it. I saw
blood. It wavered in the water like a frilly ribbon. I stepped out
and saw him kneeling by the bed. The sheet was soaked red. I
was bleeding. He started kissing the inside of my thighs, which
were blood-stained like some all-directional flower. I couldn't tell
him how happy I was with the guidebook; there was no way to
explain. Before I lost my period, like a stitch in knitting, I'd
minded blood in a prissy way, hated the bother of it, worried
about spotting. Now I could have tasted it. I felt like shouting.
That was over, the long punishment for what I'd done to myself.
I had my choices again. He was looking up at me now with
different eyes, submissive. He knelt by the bed and capped my
knees with his hands. He said words I didn't know.

Then he rampaged through the room. I found him squatting
over the guidebook. He said in English, I love you. He kept
looking up at me in this slave way. Then I understood. The
blood. He thought that meant virgin, that I'd given that to him.
'No,' I tried to tell him. 'No.' He picked me up, an arm under the
crook of my knees and one under my back. He took me to the
tub again. He was carrying me like a fragile child. I had to clear
this up. But there was no way. His brown eyes fixed. I slipped
down into the water, and heard him in the other room pulling up
his pants, the clink of keys and change. He stole out of the door.
I figured I'd never see him again and that was fine, like a sealed
perfect envelope. A tangerine peeled, every section intact. I got
up out of the water to latch the door behind him. Then I went
back to sleep, thrilling even in dream every time I felt the trickle
of blood.

The next morning, I felt proud because with the guidebook I
ordered room service coffee and it came with a wet rose on
the table-clothed tray. The petals fell off easily when I
pulled because the flower was full and seedy. Outside, the hills
were raw brown with a haze of purple on the surface. The ocean

was a plain grey colour. I took a bath and remembered the night. I sat with the coffee on the tiled rim of the tub. A line of blood ran jagged like the thinnest twig. The blood was going to be a problem. I went to the guidebook but there was nothing under Tampax. I called the desk and sat with the guidebook and finally sputtered 'Tampax' in English. The man said, 'Oh, Tampax,' and a few minutes later the elevator creaked and a boy appeared with a blue unopened box on a cloth-covered tray with a new rose. I put on a white shirt, brushed on mascara and left.

His car was parked across the street. The sight hit me like a sling. I tiptoed up: he was asleep on the back seat. He looked pathetic. He was too big for the car, and he slept with one leg folded under him and his head bent against the window. I left him be and walked downhill to ask directions at a fruit stand. I waited my turn. The high citrus smell tickled my face and behind the server two towers of orange and lemon hulls hovered. I showed him my scrap of paper with the Station Street address that the woman with the parrot had written, and he pointed. I wanted to buy lemonade but I remembered I hadn't changed my money. I started walking.

I passed a movie theatre with calligraphy on the marquee. The photographs by the ticket booth showed a huge Omar Sharif, older now, with salt and pepper hair. I had seen all his movies. I had wondered whether he was even still alive. He was never in anything any more. But his career hadn't fallen to ruins. He was here.

I heard birds as I climbed the winding streets and I smelled myrtle and sage. There was also the distant hammer sound of construction. I hadn't expected the whirring of bicycles everywhere. They were black and old, like the cars. After a few minutes outside I was used to camels. I'd stopped and touched the black lips of one, wet and soft, gumming my hand. Then I felt something nudge my hip. It was the Mercedes. At first I was mad. I twisted my skirt to see if it had made a mark. He sat at the wheel, grinning, motioning me to get in. I didn't see what else I could do, so I got in the front seat, giving up my adventure but glad anyway. I showed him the Station Street address.

He put a hand, softly, on my lower belly. I wriggled away.

But it was good he found me. He studied a map and it took us fifteen minutes of turns and curves, in opposite directions. Then we were at the house.

It still stood. A tall straggly eucalyptus waited in front. It was a wooden and concrete house, three floors with two balconies, brownish coloured with old rusty metal and stucco. The roof was red tile, Spanish looking. I saw a metal drain-pipe like the one at home. The eucalyptus moved in the wind above me. I wanted to get rid of the driver. I didn't know how long I would be. I didn't want anyone waiting for me.

I returned to the car, knocked on the window and motioned to him wildly, to say it could be a long time. He pointed to his chest, then to the floor of the car. I guess he meant that he'd be there. I shrugged, tapping my watch. I spread out my hand wide. Eternity. He folded his arms and closed his eyes.

The sky was clear blue with no clouds and I heard the drift of a slight wind in the eucalyptus leaves, a tired and very old sound. Patience, they seemed to whisper, patience. Summer is long. My heart beat like something flung against a wall. There was no bell, and I knocked. A wind chime of crude glass and metal pipes hung from the eaves. Nobody answered. The porch was cool, clay-tiled. I knocked again.

I checked my slip of paper against the number on the door. Yes, twenty-two was the number. Outside the door was an old orange plastic chair and on the ground, the dish for a plant, filled with what looked like rain-water. I heard a window shoved open in the house next door to the right, and a woman's hot fast voice spilled through and I said, 'Isam Atassi. American.' There was a noise inside her building of feet on a staircase. A door whipped open and the woman stood there looking me over.

She crossed her arms firmly over her substantial chest and spoke to me, her head shaking. The only words I recognized were 'no America, no America.' For a moment I thought she was trying to chase me away but then she was showing me into her house with her arms, almost bowing, big loops of arm hanging down like stretching dough from shoulder to elbow, from elbow to hand. She stood with her ample back to me, hands on hips, calling up the stairs; a little girl ran down, a round-limbed blue-eyed blonde. The woman said something to the child, and the child gathered her skirts in both fists and started running. 'No America,' the woman said again, this time bending in a near curtsy. I finally got it; she didn't speak English. She motioned me to sit and I did. She sat across from me and folded her hands on her lap and her feet one behind the other. I couldn't help noticing her legs. Her calves were enormous, over the dainty gesture of her feet, and patterns of black hair were trapped under her nylon stockings. Then she sprang up, graceful and light, and slowly lifted the lid off a green cut-glass bowl of candy. To be polite I took one. It was a date wrapped around nuts, and rolled in sugar and ground pistachio. It was good. She slowly pantomimed drinking from a glass, then lifted her eyebrows to ask if I wanted anything. I shook my head no, not wanting to get into a beverage charade.

We sat politely in the still living-room on fancy maroon velvet couches with gold tassels, our hands folded, looking in different directions. She smiled at me every few moments. After a long while the girl skidded in with a boy who might have been her brother but didn't look like it. They were calling back and forth in avid musical conversation. The boy stood before the woman, probably his grandmother, hands at his sides and chin down, awaiting an order. More fast Arabic. I rested with the ease of understanding absolutely nothing.

Then the boy turned to face me and said, 'I know English.'
'Oh, good,' I said, loudly, 'Are you learning in school?'
'Yes,' he said. 'School.'
'What is your name?' I said.
'My name is Nauras Awafti.'
I reached out my hand. 'My name is Mayan Atassi.'
'Yes. There are many here,' the boy said.
The grandmother became impatient and pulled the boy to her by the back of his shirt. He turned and translated for her. She fired questions at him hard and fast. Then he swiveled back to me. She smiled, and showed her teeth, some of them not white, and lifted her old plump hand in a wave.
'I am American,' I said. 'My mother is American, my father

143

is from here. Egyptian. He grew up next door. My father is Mohammed Atassi and I came here to find him.'

'Mohammed ah-yah,' the old woman said, her head going up and down. The boy translated what I had said.

'He left my mother years ago. I haven't seen my father—Mohammed—since I was twelve years old.' I marked the height with my hand. 'Around your age. I wonder if you, or your grandmother, knows where he is.'

He grinned and said, 'She's not my grandmother,' as if this were a hilarious mistake. I hoped to hell she was not his mother. 'She's my grandmother's sister. My grandmother's upstairs.' He pointed to the ceiling.

The old woman grabbed his collar again sternly to get him back to business.

'Does she know where my father is?' I repeated.

She shook her head and I knew my answer even before he translated.

'You come all the way from America to find him?' the boy said.

'Yes,' I said. The woman closed her eyes and continued rocking her head.

She spoke and the boy translated. 'He hasn't been there for a long time. Not thirty years. She says he's somewhere in America. When his father die, next door, he wasn't at funeral. You have bad luck because they live there next door, Farhan's wife and daughter. But they went for two months already to America.'

America. I was astonished. 'Where in America?' I said.

She shrugged.

'She says she doesn't know. But she thinks California.'

I looked at the little blonde girl. She was sitting in a big chair, her arms clutched to the armrests, her round legs ending in blunted sneakers. She stared up at me, the American.

The boy said that my father's mother was very old but still in the house next door. He asked if I would like to meet her.

I thought I'd heard the translation wrong. 'Yes!' I said. 'Yes!' My other grandmother.

The old woman spoke and the boy said that she had invited me to eat a meal with them first. She stood up, with her huge

144

knees facing out, bent them in a *plié* and lifted and spread her arms to encompass the room. The woman's repertoire of gestures belonged to a clown. A fat clown. I liked her very much, I appreciated her exaggerated courtesies, but I wanted to go. I tapped my watch and pointed at the house next door. I was sick of people—even Egyptians, even neighbours—who saw my father once thirty years ago. I didn't want strangers. I had a grandmother locked in the house next door.

The old woman rose, negotiated her weight around the furniture and motioned me with a plump fluid wrist to follow. The kids stood on either side of me, looking at me as if I were the strangest being they'd ever seen. We went through a mint-green kitchen, like an old-fashioned one at home, and out of the back door. The backyard went far. Three goats faced us. There was a chicken coop too, with loud dirty-white chickens. From a eucalyptus tree, an old tyre hung and the lawn was worn smooth and grassless. Past the yard and a shed was a field, just weeds, down the hill to a stand of olive trees. I knew my father must have run there.

I could have stayed. But the woman and the boy and girl were entering the next house's back door and I followed. We walked into a cellar full of vegetables and fruit in clear jars, cans with faded labels, jars of honey and vats of olive oil and sacks of grain. I picked up a jar of olives that were still attached to their branch. The woman tapped at a jar that contained something like yellow peanut butter. Her lips opened on her teeth in a large expression that strained for meaning. 'Mohammed,' she said, and moved a hand on her ample belly.

The boy translated. 'He liked that for his meal every day.' I didn't know what it was.

We entered a kitchen that looked as if it had been remodelled twenty years before, in matching black and white checks. The cupboards seemed safe and ample, the corners rounded, the surfaces used and worn. It was clean and plain. We passed into a large living-room with plush emerald-green carpeting and fancy satin and velvet couches and chairs. Gold ropes marked off parts of the room. An old inlaid chess table and some brass trays looked Middle Eastern; the mahogany console

145

stand holding an RCA colour television could have been anywhere. I stopped at some chrome-framed pictures on a shelf. The photographs showed a wedding. The bride was a full, young, curly-haired girl who looked nothing like me. There were eight pictures of her sitting in her flower-decked throne and in each one she was wearing a different dress. My father was not there. The old woman shook her head sadly, with raised eyebrows. 'Mohammed, no,' she said.

We climbed upstairs, the children ahead. The woman ascended slowly, holding the gold velvet rope that served as a banister. On the first landing, there was a family room, with another sofa and chairs, a book shelf, a standing globe, and corridors leading to more bedrooms. We started up the second stairs. Near the top, the woman called the children back. She explained something to the boy and he ran ahead, two steps at a time, arms scissoring with purpose.

We entered the top room. A young woman with her hair held back pressed by us out of the door. She stood on the landing, holding one elbow. She was wearing a nurse's uniform with a long zipper. It was a wide, low-ceilinged room, pink and white in the eaves. Outside, eucalyptus leaves fingered the window panes. The room was full of roses, their petals falling from the night table on to table-tops, the floor, the lush satin bedspread. There she was, rising from a chair with great effort, collapsing down again, an old woman with a deeply lined dark face, a mouth large as a harmonica, with many teeth and a puff of white hair. Her eyes were clear blue. She was large and short.

'Momo,' she said, her whole face crumbling over the words. She hugged me and she smelled a way I hadn't ever known an old woman to smell, warmly sweet like caramel. We sat in white, satin-cushioned chairs and the boy translated between us. She had a clear sad look when she shook her head after the boy asked if she knew where her youngest son was. She had not heard from him for ten years, she said. Her eyebrows lifted and her large mouth formed a beautiful shape. She told the boy she had not seen him for almost twenty. She lifted her hands and I went close and knelt down so she could hold my face.

She told us that when my father was a boy he liked the

animals. He was always out in the air with animals. I asked if he
had been smart. She shrugged, frowning, then slowly nodded her
head to say that she supposed so.

I moved to the small attic window. I could see the field and
the goats. My father had run there, a boy like any boy. There
was a muddy pen. A sandbox. The woman from next door tilted
her head and made a gesture that we should let the old woman
rest.

I knelt and kissed her goodbye. We walked out and she
called us back in words I didn't recognize. She'd lifted herself up
and got to a bureau. From the top drawer, open now, I saw a
thousand things—threads, thimbles, scissors, papers, cards,
scarves, veils, stockings, lipsticks, jewellery. She extracted a tiny
photograph of my father, about an inch square, black and white
with a white ruffled edge.

She gave it to me and I closed my hand around it. I couldn't
look at it until later. In the cellar again, the woman from next
door gave me the jar of what my father had liked. She pointed to
the ceiling.

'She wanted you to have,' the boy said.

Before I left I gave them the scrap of paper where the
woman with the parrot had written my address. 'You can
visit me in America someday,' I said.

'*Inshallah*,' the boy said. He copied the address down and
returned the paper to me.

I asked him what the word meant in Arabic. I'd heard it all
around me.

'God willing,' the boy said, 'in Egypt nothing for sure.
Everything is *inshallah*.'

I asked him what my name meant.

'It's just a name like other names. A common name here.'

'I thought it meant light,' I said. That's what my parents had
told me.

'No. Nora means light.'

'What about Amneh?' That was my middle name. I thought
it meant to wish.

'No. Believer.'

147

I hoped that Ramazan was still outside and we could drive back to Cairo. He would rub my back and I would fly home into the dawn. I wanted to leave. I felt like a person who had thrown a diamond ring down off a bridge and watched it disappear into the dark water. It was over, I'd lost the gamble, he'd eluded me this time for ever and now I wanted to go home. But I felt calm. I didn't care any more. I'd had my Arab experience. As I looked around me, up at the tall slow trees, I knew I'd be back another time, for different reasons.

The car was there and they walked slowly with me to it. I opened the front passenger door and the old woman rapped her knuckles on the window of the back seat and pointed.

I shrugged. 'It's OK.'

Ramazan, who had just woken up, slumped over the steering wheel. He looked up from his dropped head like a yoked animal. The old woman kept rapping; she seemed upset. Ramazan pointed to the back seat. I got out and went in the back. I didn't understand, but I wanted to go. I rolled down the back window and looked for a moment at the house and the yard beyond, the three goats, their black heads, the shimmering yellow-green weeds of the plain field. It was as shabby as my grandmother's house in Wisconsin, the land as old. I was sad over how many different lives there were and we only got once.

Ramazan explained with the guidebook. 'Rich,' he said and he looked at me, nodding his head. He said the word again, repeating to memorize. I shook my head. He persisted. The wind tore through the open windows. My mother had always told me we were royalty over here. I laughed out loud. Twenty-two Station Street was a good house, but it wasn't royal anywhere in the world. The car stopped: I didn't know why. There was a small stand of dusty olive trees by the side of the road. Ramazan got out and I heard him pee on the dry leaves. Below him was an old stone amphitheatre. I came up behind him, toppled him, and we lay there on the cool stone, toying. I hurt my back once on a eucalyptus button.

'Greco-Roman,' he said, pointing to the stage below. It was a small, perfectly tiered circle. There was life there once.

'Arabs have everything, huh?'

'No, Egyptians.' He tapped his chest. 'We have got pyramids. Antiquities. History.' He made a sound by letting air out of his mouth.

When I put my underwear on again, the good pair, drops of blood trickled to the cotton, staining like a watercolour. I found the last scrap of paper from my wallet, on which the woman with the parrot had written that I was looking for my father who might be in Alexandria and that I hadn't seen him for seventeen years. I gave it to Ramazan. He spent a long time reading it.

In the car his face took on a new cast and he lost the plot of his smile. His hands stayed on the wheel, not playful any more. I showed him the word in the book that means airport. I made wing motions with my arms, pointed at myself—'Me, America.' We drove a long time keeping the silence and arrived in Cairo. On the way to the airport, he drove through a district of mansions on the Nile. They had domed towers, minarets, columns and mosaics, like mosques. They looked a thousand years old, or older. This was the royalty of Egypt.

'Heliopolis,' he said. He stopped before one mansion and pointed. 'Omar Sharif.'

At the airport, he came into the terminal with me. I studied the English television screen. There was a flight in the evening at eight o'clock. It was only three. He took my hand and I followed him to a phone booth. He was carrying my pack again and it felt easy to let him. It was a modern phone booth. He lifted a book, paged through, found a spot and showed me. I remembered from his hand that Arabic scans from right to left.

His hand brailled over the whole page. 'Atassi,' he said. 'Atassi. Atassi. Atassi.'

I smiled and shook my head. It was too late for that. I wanted to go home. I sat on his lap. I didn't want to close the book over a page of Atassis. He ripped the page out, folded it up, put it in my backpack, zipped the zipper. We had time to eat. He drove me to a neighbourhood of low two-storey tenement buildings. Children played in the bare street. The restaurant was small and underground, and we sat cross-legged on the floor. A short-stemmed pink rose leaned in a tin can on our table. Two of the petals, cleft in the centre, had fallen to the cloth. Light slanted into the room from back and front. Ramazan ordered in Arabic and I sat low against a pillow. We looked at each other and sometimes smiled, sometimes didn't; we had stopped trying to use words. The food began to come and set our clock. Olives and new cheese, then kibbe, then my father's layered pancake with a different butter and burnt sugar. He'd always talked about the Bedouin food, about sleeping outside with them as a boy, the open fires in the morning. The pancake tasted of honey and deep caramel and rose water. I handed Ramazan a pencil and paper for the name. He drew and whispered: 'Fatir.'

Then we used the guidebook. He pointed to his chest and showed me the word 'poor'. I smiled a little, embarrassed for him. He didn't have to ask me. I'd already decided to give him all the money I had and save only twenty dollars for the bus home from the airport. He pointed to himself again, made wing motions and said, in an accent I'd never heard, 'America.' He pointed to me and I smiled. I gave him my address, and he put it in the little bag he had around his neck where he kept money, and clasped it shut. He took my left hand and banded a cleft rose petal over my third finger. I knew before looking in the book. 'Marrying,' he said. I got up to leave. He's so young, I was thinking.

It was still light when we walked outside. I wanted to buy a souvenir. We had more than an hour. With the guidebook I showed him the word for bazaar and I shrugged. We walked into a district of close streets and corners, brown buildings and smells of burning meat. We came to a square filled with market stands and around the sides were the neon-lit fronts of casinos. He pulled me over to the edge of the square, where there was a tiled drinking fountain and a man standing with a camera draped in black cloth and a camel tied to a palm. He spoke and seemed to be asking if I wanted to have my picture taken with the camel.

We surveyed the stands of the bazaar. From a dusty market table, we picked out an everyday Turkish coffee pot, a little one. I wanted to open the jar of what my father had liked. When the woman had given it to me, I thought I'd save it for my father and give it to him as a present the first time I saw him, if I ever found him and we met again. But I didn't want to wait. I'd waited and saved enough for him. The lid stuck. I gave it to Ramazan. He held it against his belly, straining, and again I thought, he's young, and then it was open. It was a rich distilled paste that tasted of almonds and honey. We ate it with our fingers as we walked past fabric bolts and animals that licked our hands. We finished the whole jar. I turned my back for a moment and he bought me a dress. I had been staring at a painted wooden cut-out of a bride and groom propped outside a casino called The Monte Carlo. The heads were open circles for people to stand in and have their picture taken. BE THE BRIDE, it said.

In the airport I bought a snowball paperweight that showed a scene with camels and tents in the desert. Ramazan paid for it. He'd paid for the coffee pot, for dinner, for the dress, and he'd tried to pay for the wedding photographs. We passed a bar called The Ramadan Room, where an orchestrated version of 'Home of the Brave' was playing. At the departure gate I tried to give him my money. I had two hundred and ten dollars in cash. I wanted to give him all of it. He wouldn't take it. I pushed the crinkled bills into his pockets. His mouth got hard; his chin made a clean line; he took it all, balled it, jammed it down in my pack.

At the metal security bar we drank a long goodbye kiss. His articulate hands moved around my face as if fashioning an imaginary veil there.

'Goodbye,' I said. I knew absolutely that I would never see him again.

He said words I didn't understand but I made out Allah. Everything in his language had to do with God.

Wit.

Ideas.

Style.

Good Writing.

That's Esquire.

GEOFFREY BIDDLE
ALPHABET CITY

When I first worked there, the neighbourhood was not called Alphabet City. It was the Puerto Rican part of Lower East Side and the Puerto Ricans called it Loisaida, low-ee-SIGH-da, a New York-Puerto Rican version of Lower East Side.

Loisaida is bounded to the north by Fourteenth Street and to the south by Houston, which falls one below First Street but is still two miles from the bottom of Manhattan. From Avenue A in the west the neighbourhood runs east across Avenue B and Avenue C—through rows of five-storey tenements built in the mid-nineteenth century for immigrants—across Avenue D, through the public housing projects built in the late 1940s and early 1950s, across the footbridges that span East River Drive, across its long, thin park, to the East River.

The Puerto Ricans started to come in the late 1940s when the neighbourhood was Jewish. They dominated Loisaida in 1977, when I first started taking pictures there. I gave away pictures and got to know people. I went to clubs, to parties, to events and into homes. Some people helped me; some tried to make me leave. After two years, I couldn't make the pictures say any more, so I stopped.

In 1987, the pictures won the Essay of the Year Award from the University of Missouri School of Journalism, and I became interested in working with the material again. I returned to the neighbourhood with my pictures and found many of the people I had photographed. I interviewed them and took new pictures of them. This story presents the old and the new together.

Alphabet City is a name that was popularized by real-estate developers in the mid-1980s when property prices rose and tenements became condominiums, a process which is slowly continuing. The Puerto Ricans still say Loisaida, and the city has given Avenue C the additional name Loisaida Avenue, but the new people, and people from outside the neighbourhood, use the name Alphabet City.

I ris Chiquita: I'm no more Iris Chiquita. Now I'm just Iris. You see that lady? That's too much fatter? My husband lives with this lady now. *Verdad*. She was my best friend. Oh, shit. That's no fair no how.

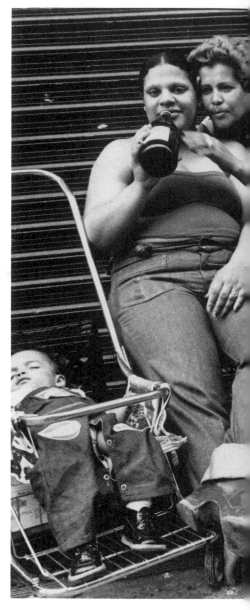

1977. Iris Chiquita is standing behind 'Iris Grande', who is holding a bottle.

Amy Zapata: I'm twenty-three now. Then I was twelve. My mother had money. She had a friend that owned a beauty parlour and they hooked her up with this job. She used to go to Peru, Spain, and come to New York City with drugs taped to her body. She came home with a lot of hundred-dollar bills. Then after that she started shooting up drugs.

One day, she brought a man to the house. They did whatever. She left him sleeping and stole his wallet. The man could have raped me or my sisters, could've hurt us. That's when I found out my mother didn't really care about us. So that night, I went to this place and worked all night bagging up dope and coke. When I made enough money, I called my aunt in Puerto Rico, got the tickets right in the airport and sent my sisters off.

My mom's in prison. She looks good but she has AIDS. She used to sleep in abandoned buildings. She used to use the vein in her neck. Any vein she could find in her body.

Above: 1988. Amy Zapata (right) with her sister Lillian.

Opposite: 1977. Amy Zapata (front right). Lillian is standing against the wall.

Pistol: My moms was a good person. She cared. The day she died, she told me that my father hit her, and I told her: that was good for you, for not cooking for him. And she left. I didn't know she took the pills. They told me that it wasn't my fault. I still think I was responsible though. She came to me to help her, to, how they call it, calm her down, comfort her. But I didn't. I just started breaking on her. The last thing she said was, OK, you want to be on his side? Stay with him. Like she knew it was going to happen.

Hah. I want a copy of this one. [Opposite]. I was about sixteen years old, I think. I figured I was bad in the street, so I guess that's why I wanted to buy a gun for my son, so he could protect himself when he grows up, so nobody fuck with him.

Then I started thinking that's wrong, you have to be a maniac to buy a gun for a kid like that. I talked to a couple of people and they made me sell it. They taught me something, you know?

Above: 1978. Pistol with his mother and younger brother.
Opposite: 1978. James, Pistol's son.

very issue of Granta features fiction, politics, travel writing, photography and more.
o don't miss out — subscribe today and save up to 40% from the £6.99 cover price.

Name _____

Address _____

_____

Postcode _____

BI371B

If I subscribe for 3 years, I save £33.93.
That's a 40% saving.

I want to ❑ enter ❑ renew my subscription
(4 issues per year) to Granta:
❑ 1 yr £19.95 ❑ 2 yrs £37.00 ❑ 3 yrs £49.95.
Start my subscription with issue number _____

Payment: ❑ Cheque enclosed
❑ Access/American Express/Visa/Diners Club
Expiry Date _____

[| | | | | | | | | | | | | | | | | |]

Signature _____

Overseas postage:
Europe: Please add £6 per year.
Outside Europe: £12 per year air-speeded, £20 per year airmail.

Please tick this box if you do not want to receive direct mail from other companies ❑

---

want to ❑ enter ❑ renew my own subscription:
1 yr £19.95 ❑ 2 yrs £37.00 ❑ 3 yrs £49.95.

ne _____

dress _____

_____

Postcode _____

art my subscription with issue number _____
yment: ❑ Cheque enclosed
Access/American Express/Visa/Diners Club

[| | | | | | | | | | | | | | | | | |]

p.____Signature_____

____total for ___ gifts and ❑ my own subscription.

I want to give a one year £19.95 gift subscription to:

ne _____

dress _____

_____

Postcode _____

erseas postage:
rope: Please add £6 per year.
tside Europe: £12 per year air-speeded, £20 per
ar airmail.

ase tick this box if you do not want to receive direct
il from other companies ❑

Name _____

Address _____

_____

Postcode _____

BI37GB

FREEPOST
2-3 Hanover Yard
Noel Road
London
N1 8BR

FREEPOST
2-3 Hanover Yard
Noel Road
London
N1 8BR

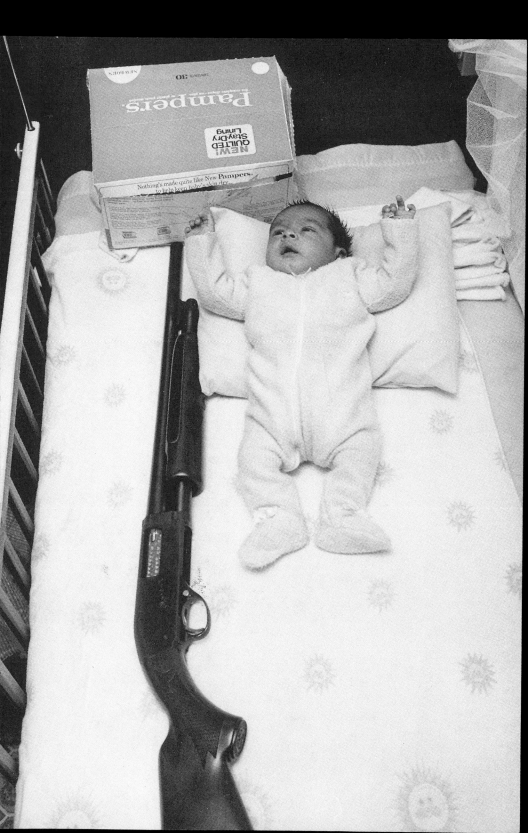

Julio Rivera, boxing trainer (not in photograph): Shadow. Making shadow. He has no boxing shoes. He's got cheap tennis. Cheap pants, too. Flat-footed. Too wide open. No balance. He's an amateur fighter, you can see. He's a poor guy. He's a beginner, with dreams.

1977. Lower East Side Boxing Club.

Carmelo Negron (not in photograph): Look at the faces. There's a lot of dreams. Like, I'm getting out of this place. They should just do it the smart way. What I did, I trusted my trainer too much. We were big time, and he just bugged out. It takes a lot more than skill. You can't trust anyone when you're in the business of making money in boxing.

1978. Lower East Side Boxing Club.

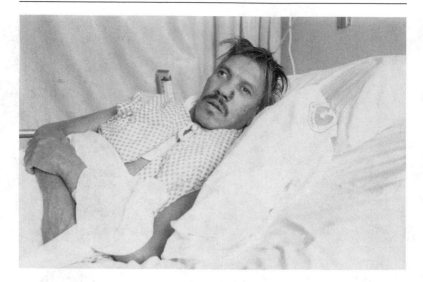

Ariel Velez: Who told you that? A woman? A guy? You ask the doctor. I would know if I have AIDS. It's some different place. My appetite is normal. Everything is normal.

My history? I was in drugs, then I start trying to be a boxer, but I blew it. I tried to kick it, but I couldn't. I wanted all my life to be a boxer. That's my one ambition.

Above: 1988. Ariel Velez in Cabrini Medical Centre.
Opposite: 1978. Ariel Velez is the boxer on the left.

E lizabeth 'Bam-Bam' Ortiz: Oh, my God. Look at Alex! That's my son! I look like I want to kill somebody. And Nellie. She looks beat. Joe. This bum. Wow. The way years go by.

I was addicted for fourteen years. I was on the street for seven and a half years. I didn't have a place to live. I had my mother, but once you leave momma's house you don't know how to go back. She had my son with her. I was wild. I was banging. I loved heroin. It's amazing that I got off it. And without no help. My mother sent me away for a while and I kicked it on my own.

Now I have an apartment and my son is with me. And I'm happy, because now I can really keep an eye on him. Before I couldn't.

1978. Elizabeth Ortiz is second from the left. Her son is at the back in a check shirt.

Luis Solie: If your rooster's good—and mine is good—we can make a fight with five, ten thousand dollars. All the people know the place to go. We can start at ten o'clock, and we finish the next morning at seven o'clock.

Sometimes the fights are only one minute, two minutes. Whatever the judge says counts. In a big money fight, they have to fight all the way to their death. Or until one runs away. If it lasts twenty minutes, that's a draw. Nobody loses anything.

When they fight, they jump. If you know about roosters, you know when one throws out his leg. You don't see it, because it's too fast. But I see it. Sometimes they hit the vein. I know, in a minute, the blood will start to come out. Then this rooster can't go far. That's when we bet. You have to be very smart, if you like to be at cockfights.

Above: 1988. Luis Solie (right), with Roman.

Opposite: 1978. Luis is in the white shirt, behind Roman, who is pointing.

Richard Morales: HTC. Homeboys Together Chilling. And when we used to fight, we used to be Hard To Control. There was a good twenty-five, thirty of us. We didn't bother with the drug dealers, just with the young kids like us who thought they were bad: staring at us, or throwing our girls a kiss. As many as we catch, we just beat them up. Payback time all the time.

Now I go to college, with three others. I know I was doing wrong, but the way it was out here, that was something to be proud of.

1977. Richard Morales is in the striped shirt.

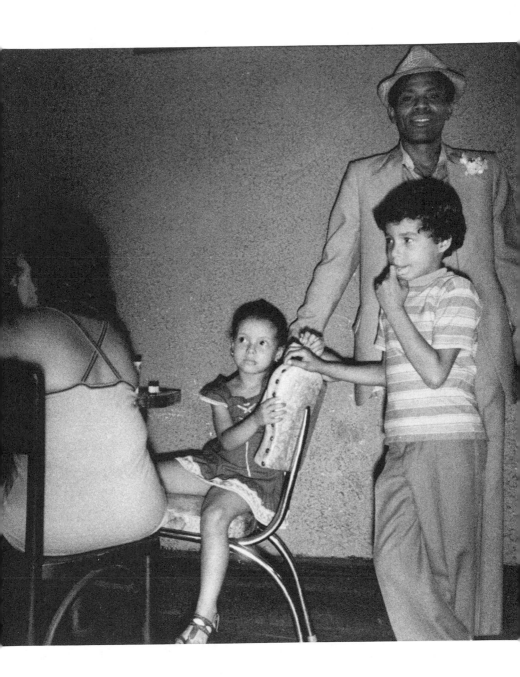

Tito Roman: I was with her. Me and the girl you have in the picture, Linda. On the right, with our boy Tito. I met her in Puerto Rico when I was running a taxi. I drove her from one town to the other, in the morning and in the afternoons. She was in school and I was old enough for her, because she was fourteen and I was twenty-eight. We settled up together and we had three boys, the last one here in New York. She was all right. She helped me a lot. Then she started to have an affair with a Cuban guy, so we split. She kept all three boys.

After that, I saw her hanging around downtown. And then I saw my boys sleeping in the street, the hallway, under the steps, hungry, no shoes. She had started using dope. Me and my new wife won the three boys through the courts.

I heard she's still in pretty bad shape. I haven't seen her for three or four years. I heard that she was pregnant by a Dominican guy, in Puerto Rico, somewhere in San Juan. I don't know where.

Above: 1988. Luis Roman with his son Tito.
Opposite: 1978. Tito on his mother's lap.

SEAMUS DEANE
CRAIGAVON BRIDGE

Father Regan was lighting a candle in his dark classroom at the foot of the statue of the Blessed Virgin. Regan permitted no overhead lights when he gave his formal religious address at the beginning of our last year in school. Regan was small, neat, economical. After he said 'Boys,' he stopped for a bit and looked at us. Then he dropped his eyes and kept them down until he said, more loudly this time, 'Boys.' He had complete silence this time.

'Some of you here, one or two of you perhaps, know the man I am going to talk about today. You may not know you know him, but that doesn't matter.

'More than thirty years ago, during the troubles in Derry, this man was arrested and charged with the murder of a policeman. The policeman had been walking home one night over Craigavon Bridge. It was a bleak night, November, nineteen hundred and twenty-two. The time was two in the morning. The policeman was off duty; he was wearing civilian clothes. There were two men coming the other way, on the other side of the bridge. As the policeman neared the middle of the bridge, these two men crossed over to his side. They were strolling, talking casually. They had their hats pulled down over their faces and their coat collars turned up for it was wet and cold. As they passed the policeman, one of them said "Goodnight" and the policeman returned the greeting. And then suddenly he found himself grabbed from behind and lifted off his feet. He tried to kick but one of the men held his legs. "This is for Neil McLaughlin," said one. "May you rot in the hell you're going to, you murdering bastard." They lifted him to the parapet and held him there for a minute like a log and let him stare down at the water—seventy, eighty feet below. Then they pushed him over and he fell, with the street lights shining on his wet coat until he disappeared into the shadows with a splash. They heard him thrashing and he shouted once. Then he went under. His body was washed up three days later. No one saw them. They went home and they said nothing.

'A week later a man was arrested and charged with the murder. He was brought to trial. But the only evidence the police had was that he was the friend and workmate of Neil

Photo: Chris Steele-Perkins (Magnum)

179

McLaughlin, who had been murdered by a policeman a month before. The story was that, before McLaughlin died on the street where he had been shot, coming out of the newspaper office where he worked, he had whispered the name of his killer to this man who had been arrested. And this man had been heard to swear revenge, to get the policeman—let's call him Mahon—in revenge for his friend's death. There was no point in going to the law, of course; justice would never be done; everyone knew that, especially in those years. So maybe the police thought they could beat an admission out of him, but he did not flinch from his story. That night he was not even in the city. He had been sent by his newspaper to Letterkenny twenty miles away, and he had several witnesses to prove it. The case was thrown out. People were surprised, even though they believed the man to be innocent. Innocence was no guarantee for a Catholic then. Nor is it now.

'Well, I wasn't even in the city in those days. But I met this man several times and we became friendly. I was then a young curate and this man was prominent in local sporting circles and he helped in various ways to raise money for the parish building fund. One night, in the sacristy of the Long Tower Church, just down the road from here, he told me that he had not been to confession in twenty years. He had something on his conscience that no penance could relieve. I told him to trust in God's infinite mercy; I offered to hear his confession; I offered to find someone else, a monk I knew down in Portglenone, to whom he could go, in case he did not want to confess to me. But no, he wouldn't go. No penance, he said, would be any use, because, in his heart, he could not feel sorrow for what he had done. But he wanted to tell someone, not as a confession, but in confidence.

'So he told me about being arrested. He told me about the beatings he had been given—rubber truncheons, punches, kicks, threats to put him over the bridge. He told me how he had resisted these assaults and never wavered.

'"Oh," said I, "that's just a testimony to the strength you get from knowing you are in the right."

'He looked at me in amazement. "D'ye think that's what I wanted to tell you? The story of my innocence? For God's sake,

Father, can't you see? I wasn't innocent. I was guilty. I killed Mahon and I'd kill him again if he came through that door this minute. That's why I can't confess. I have no sorrow, no resolve not to do it again. No pity. Mahon shot my best friend dead in the street, for nothing. He was a drunken policeman with a gun, looking for a Teague to kill, and he left that man's wife with two young children and would have got off scot-free for the rest of his days, probably promoted for sterling service. And Neil told me as he lay there, with the blood draining from him, that Mahon did it. 'Billy Mahon, Billy Mahon, the policeman,' that's what he said. And even then, I had to run back into the doorway and leave his body there in the street because they started shooting down the street from the city walls. And I'm not sorry I got Mahon and I told him what it was for before I threw him over that bridge and he knew, just too late, who I was when I said 'Goodnight' to him. It was goodnight all right. One murdering bastard less."

'Boys, that man went to the grave without confessing that sin. And think of all the wrongs that were done in that incident. Two men were murdered. Two men—three, for there was another man whose name was never mentioned—were murderers. Indeed maybe there was another murderer, for it's possible that Mahon was not the policeman involved. And there were perjurers who swore that the accused was elsewhere that night. And there were policemen who assaulted a man in custody. And there were judges who would certainly have acquitted any policeman, no matter how guilty, and would have found guilty any Catholic, no matter how innocent, on the slightest shred of evidence. The whole situation makes men evil. Evil men make the whole situation. And these days, similar things occur. Some of you boys may feel like getting involved when you leave school, because you sincerely believe that you would be on the side of justice, fighting for the truth. But, boys, let me tell you, there is a judge who sees all, knows all and is never unjust; there is a judge whose punishments and rewards are beyond the range of human imagining; there is a Law greater than the laws of human justice, far greater than the law of revenge, more enduring than the laws of any state whatsoever. That Judge is God, that Law is God's

Law and the issue at stake is your immortal soul.

'We live, boys, in a world that will pass away. The shadows that candle throws upon the walls of this room are as substantial as we. Injustice, tyranny, freedom, national independence are realities that will fade too, for they are not ultimate realities and the only life worth living is a life lived in the light of the ultimate. I know there are some who believe that the poor man who committed that murder was justified, and that he will be forgiven by an all-merciful God for what he did. That may be. I fervently hope that it is so, for who would judge God's mercy? But it is true too of the policeman; he may have been as plagued by guilt as his own murderer; he may have justified himself too; he may have refused sorrow and known no peace of mind; he may have forgiven himself or he may have been forgiven by God. It is not for us to judge. But it is for us to distinguish, to see the difference between wrong done to us and equal wrong done by us; to know that our transient life, no matter how scarred, how broken, how miserable it may be, is also God's miracle and gift; that we may try to improve it, but we may not destroy it. If we destroy it in another, we destroy it in ourselves. Boys, as you enter upon your last year with us, you are on the brink of entering a world of wrong, insult, injury, unemployment, a world where the unjust hold power and the ignorant rule. But there is an inner peace nothing can reach; no insult can violate, no corruption can deprave. Hold to that; it is what your childish innocence once was and what your adult maturity must become. Hold to that. I bless you all.'

And he raised his hand and made the sign of the Cross above our heads and crossed the room, blew out the candle as the bell rang wildly in the chapel tower, and asked that the light be switched on. He left in silence with the candle smoking heavily behind him at the foot of the statue, stubby in its thick drapery of wax.

'That was your grandfather,' said McShane to me. 'I know that story too.'

I derided him. I had heard the story too, but I wasn't going to take it on before everyone else. Anyway, it was just folklore. I had heard it when I was much younger and lay on the landing at night listening to the grown-ups talking in the kitchen below and had leaned over the banisters and imagined it was the edge of the parapet and that I was falling, falling down to the river of the hallway, as deaf and shining as a log.

In February of this year the Tory party chairman, Chris Patten, gave a long interview. In the carefully coded language that Tory grandees use on occasions like this, he hinted at the government's change of thinking on Europe. It proved to be the opening shot in a long bout of Conservative infighting on the question of the EC and a single European currency.

Which magazine did he choose to air these differences in? There was no choice, *Marxism Today* ran the interview.

Quite simply, *Marxism Today* is _the_ forum for intellectual, political and cultural debate in the United Kingdom.

GIORGIO PRESSBURGER
THE LAW OF
WHITE SPACES

S ome years ago I resolved to research the lives and careers of a number of doctors I had known when I was a child. I was in relatively good health at the time, and that fact enabled me to view the individuals with a certain distance, far removed from the terror with which I had regarded them as a boy.

I studied the contents of the personal archives of Professor S, a history scholar and a man of great intellectual and moral honesty. He had decided, a long time before, to conduct research along the same lines as mine, but with a quite different aim. During our brief conversation seven years ago, I was able to establish that for Professor S, medicine, and indeed science in general—notwithstanding the huge advances made in the last few decades—represented 'the darkness born of the light.' I well remember his exact words, and those of his hasty correction: 'or rather, the light that feeds on the darkness.'

The voice of Professor S was very hoarse at the time and I had to strain to hear him. But my discomfort was nothing against the compassion he showed towards those modest doctors who, in the course of their careers, had been forced to try their strength against 'mysteries bigger than themselves.'

He lent me the papers relating to the case described in the pages that follow. I have summarized them as best I could.

One winter morning Doctor Abraham Fleischmann realized that he could no longer remember the name of his best friend. He was alone in the house; his housekeeper only came in on week-days, and his old friend Lea was confined to her bed with a severe migraine. In the night the doctor had dreamed about an earthquake, and after that about a meeting with a curious individual whose hair shone with brilliantine and whom everyone referred to as the Spirit of the Times. In the morning when he awoke his thoughts turned to his friend, a television announcer and a master of chess.

He had never written down his friend's telephone number in his leather-bound address book, nor stored it in the memory of the personal computer that was a present from his cousin in Connecticut; he phoned his friend every day. But in November the friend had left for a four-week holiday, and between then and now his telephone number had erased itself from Doctor Fleischmann's memory.

He went to look it up in the telephone directory—but under what name? For more than ten minutes the doctor was unable to recall either the first or the last name of Isaac Rosenwasser. 'I'll just see if I'm still asleep,' he said, pinching his arm. 'Of course, this might be only a dream too,' he went on, loudly. 'Dreaming of pinching oneself; what nonsense,' he thought.

Fleischmann set great store by the discipline, by the almost stately formality of his own thought processes. He was a person who managed to find the appropriate saying for every occasion, and his patients, as well as praising him as a great doctor, considered him a veritable master of life.

'What is his name?' he persisted to himself that cold morning. 'It's here on the tip of my tongue, and yet I cannot remember it. This is ridiculous—we grew up together!'

Before long his indignation turned to fear, timidly at first, then more violent. 'What if it's the beginning of a disease?' He banished the thought. 'Don't go assuming the worst just because of a simple memory lapse. The synapses of two neurones got a bit mixed up. An ion of sodium or potassium missed the boat between two cells in the cerebral cortex.'

He got out of bed and did a few gymnastic exercises. At

fifty-five he was in the prime of life, fit enough on the ski slopes to leave many younger men behind. He had more than one lover among the younger, more forward women of the Eighth District, even among the girls. He telephoned one of them, and during their afternoon encounter in a tiny apartment he was able to forget his disagreeable case of amnesia.

But five days later Doctor Fleischmann was surprised to find himself searching at length and in vain for the word 'injection': the sounds escaped him. He stood speechless before his patient. The word's meaning was circulating in the convolutions of his brain but its sound would not come. After twenty long seconds the doctor found it again in his acoustic memory. He wrote the patient a prescription for injections of vitamin B12 to be taken once a day for a week.

'I'm so tired!' Fleischmann exclaimed loudly, as soon as the patient had closed the door behind him. 'Perhaps I too ought to take a cure for my nerves. I have too many commitments. I need to sort things out.' At that stage it hadn't occurred to him that he might possibly be dealing with an organic illness. He was sure in himself of the machinery of his body; his daily performances, at sport and in bed, convinced him that it was functioning perfectly.

He wasted no time in attempting to reassure himself that all was well: in an exercise that, while a little childish, was quite typical of him, he repeated to himself a hundred times the word 'injection', each time scrutinizing every thought and mental association that passed through his head. In this way he alighted on the thought of death, and beyond it, of nothing. For an instant he felt like he was dying. 'It's obviously a case of an irreversible deterioration of the brain cells,' he thought on the subject of his unexpected amnesia, something that had never occurred to him before then. He began to sweat and felt an emptiness in his stomach. So, he thought, the pencil was poised over his name; soon he was to be scored off the list of the living and would end up, limbs rigid, on the marble slab of some dissecting room.

Without thinking, he made an appointment at an analysis clinic for the next day, and at seven in the morning he went to have blood and urine samples taken. 'It's not as if I'm waiting to be sentenced,' he thought as he came out of the clinic. 'The judgement was pronounced long ago, the moment I was cast among the living. It won't matter if one day I can no longer pronounce the word "I", because the "I" will no longer exist, or it will be unable to speak. I won't care.'

He went straight away to see the patients waiting for him. During his visits he noticed with triumphant bitterness that the number of words disappearing from his vocabulary for seconds, for hours at a time was increasing; it was becoming ridiculous. And no longer was it just words with complicated sounds, like plantigrade or clepsydra; even everyday terms, like toothpaste or sand, were beginning to obstruct momentarily the flow of thought in his brain. 'I'm worse and deteriorating by the minute,' thought Fleischmann. 'But it will pass. I'll get used to it.'

He went to his wife's house and spent a long time talking with her about trivial things. He was astonished at how sharp and alert he felt. It was as if he had only begun to live from the moment his life had been put in danger. Before, he'd always seemed to be living in a memory, as if in a larval state, a blind thing, completely bereft of consciousness. Now, even his astonishment struck him as an emotion he had never experienced before.

Two days passed in this way. On the third day he went to get the results of his tests. There was a significant alteration in his blood analysis. Three or four values were quite a bit above their normal limits and, left alone, would soon have caused Doctor Fleischmann to have what his colleagues called a Turn. In fact, as he was giving him the written results of the tests Flebus asked him, 'Have you had a Turn yet? Do you stammer now and again? Get a bit tongue-tied? Have difficulty getting the words out?' Fleischmann denied that he had. He went home, shut himself in his study and cried.

That evening, with his elbows resting on a clean table-cloth, he looked long and hard at his son, his mother, his wife, all of whom had remained living together after he had moved out. 'Does any of this make sense?' He was coming to realize with horror that everything he cared most about—love, affection, responsibility for the lives of his dear ones—was deserting him, leaving him in mocking conversation with a world that was a stranger.

'You look pale, Papa,' said his son Benjamin. 'You're taking on too many patients. Perhaps if you wrote fewer prescriptions for purgatives and tried to enjoy life a bit more . . .' Fleischmann knocked over his bowl of soup and stormed out. As he went he saw a terrified, hunted look on the faces of his wife and son.

In People's Theatre Street the evening was cool and full of sounds. The drunks were coming out of the wine cellars on all fours. Fleischmann tried talking some courage into his tortured self. 'Who said the suppositions of science were absolute truths? The human brain is immense: the size of two continents, two planets, two universes. I'll find some way out of this. My time has not yet come.'

He enrolled in a speed reading and memory course that was being held in a dark two-roomed apartment on Joseph II Street.

On the first evening, climbing the blackened staircase of the five-storey building, he met a group of unshaven young people and some fastidious office workers determined to get on in life, all dressed in more or less the same fashion in rough and shoddy clothes. Inside the apartment, on its creaky wooden floor, twenty or so chairs and a table were set out in a manner intended to lend a serious air to the proceedings. This was one of the first private enterprises allowed by the State. 'So the State permits the use of memory!' he thought. 'Quite. The State is all memory. And like all other memories it is destined to destroy itself.'

A few weeks into the course he noticed a significant improvement in his ability to remember faces, names and places of recent acquaintance (remote events had been preserved intact in his memory and in his forgetfulness). The atmosphere that reigned in the class made him feel as if they were initiates of some sect whose duty was to continue life on earth after the Catastrophe. Reading at speed, across the page, backwards and forwards, up and down, using techniques based on the combined use of the senses and on hypnosis; to Fleischmann these were what would sustain him for the rest of his life, what would make it liveable and free from the shame of physical decay. The three weeks of the course were the last bearable moments of the illustrious doctor's existence.

When the course ended he received a diploma, and the professor—a small, fair, insignificant-looking man who had learned the techniques of memory in England—heaped praise upon him. Never had he come across a pupil so diligent, and at the same time blessed with so much intelligence.

Fleischmann took up his work again full of optimism. He criss-crossed the back streets of the Eighth District, visiting dark apartments and making calls on pensioners with bad hearts and on ninety-year-old women resigned to loneliness. He was full of the conviction that he had something important to offer them: a few minutes of life.

One day returning from his rounds he heard the telephone ring while he was still at the bottom of the stairs. He ran up the remaining steps. He was not in the habit of hurrying, and indeed he hated the phone for the way it enabled the most unforeseen cases of life and death to reach him, of all people, at any time of the day or night. He hadn't considered that when he had decided to pursue a career in medicine. When he opened the door he found his housekeeper—a thin, deaf eighty-year-old—already holding out the receiver to him with tears in her eyes. 'Come in, come in, doctor,' whispered the little old lady. 'It's for you.'

This is how Abraham Fleischmann learned of his brother's death. Like him a doctor, professor of comparative anatomy and a surgeon of international repute, his brother had always had something of a delicate constitution. But his death was a surprise. 'A stroke, or a heart-attack . . .' Fleischmann murmured to himself with a professional objectivity. A moment later he let out such a painful wail that the old woman fled. The doctor left the house and ran down Kun Street, sobbing loudly and choking on his own tears. A few passers-by turned to stare, but left him alone.

Abraham Fleischmann had loved and admired his brother in

adulthood. When they were children, however, he had found his brother's melancholy and introspective manner irritating. At that age he wasn't capable of recognizing what gentleness and depth of feeling lay hidden behind his listlessness. Now his brother lay in hospital, wrapped in a sheet. He had been dead for half an hour and under the folds of linen Fleischmann could just make out his features, the protrusion of his nose, the shape of his mouth. And though he was used to attending to the dead and the dying, the sight had the same effect on him as it has on other men. A cry rose to his lips: 'Why? Why? Why?'

The doctor sobbed and moaned, his face running with tears, but inside he was accusing his brother of being in some way improvident, of having consented to death, of having wanted it. And even then he already knew that, within a few days, he would have yielded to the superior wisdom and mildness of his late brother, whose wish for death—for why else should one so young and so wise have fallen ill?—was simply another expression of that great good sense. To Fleischmann, staying alive now seemed an act of unparalleled foolishness, and the whole world nothing more than a huge, filthy slaughterhouse.

He spotted his sister-in-law hiding in a window bay in the hospital corridor. From her he learned that his brother had been ill for a long time, a number of years, and that purely out of regard for his mother—herself suffering from the infirmities of old age—he had hidden the full extent of his illness from everyone.

The day before he died he had summoned all his strength and telephoned his mother, and when she had asked him how he was, he had told her without hesitation and in a steady voice that he was fine. Then he had said his goodbyes to her, saying that he was off on a long journey but would be back in a few months. There wasn't a hint of self-pity in his voice. Hanging up the receiver he stared long and hard at the wall before whispering, 'In five or six months' time, once she's got used to my absence, tell her everything. Look after her.'

As he listened to this story, Fleischmann was overcome with emotion; he felt a radiance. It was as if he were present at some

193

great and solemn event. Then came the moment of truth. First, his sister-in-law asked him to go to her house and fetch the clothes to dress the corpse in, telling him in which chest he would find them. There was a short silence. 'Do you still remember the prayer for the dead?' she asked, timidly. 'You have to recite it. If you don't remember it, learn it tonight. It's about twenty lines long. You have to do it. For him. I'm sure you'll manage.'

Doctor Fleischmann left the hospital in great agitation. It was beginning to seem as if his brother's fate depended on him, on his ability, or lack of it, to learn the prayer for the dead. 'Just now that my memory's in ruins!' he laughed in desperation. 'What nonsense. He's gone and that's that.'

He went to his brother's house, fetched the clothes and took them back to the hospital; then he went to his wife's and mother's house, saying nothing about his brother's death to them, according to the wishes of the deceased, and finally he returned home. He asked his housemaid to find him the old ivory-bound prayer book, its title page covered with the scrawled names of his ancestors and the dates on which they had died.

That evening he didn't eat. He sat down in his dark and dusty study and placed the prayer book in front of him on the writing desk. How long had it been since he had held that book in his hands? Thirty years? Forty? Why did he have to pretend to subscribe to rituals which he had always found childish and incomprehensible? Life and death, the doctor realized, made no more sense to him than those prayers.

He opened the book. The square-shaped characters appeared completely unfamiliar to him. The whole system of transliteration seemed stupidly complicated and arbitrary. 'Still, I don't suppose there's much point in starting to pick holes in the alphabet. It's an old-fashioned invention, I know, but right now there's not much of an alternative.'

With the help of a transcription into the Roman alphabet, Fleischmann began to decipher the prayer word by word. But then he decided to memorize the text using the old square characters. Through all this, the meaning of the words remained completely obscure to him. 'It doesn't matter,' he thought. 'Even my father who could recite all the prayers so fluently didn't know the meaning of a single word he pronounced. I'll pretend I'm learning a musical score.' He began to repeat the useless and necessary sounds of the words over to himself, slowly at first, in brief snatches, and then, with growing confidence, more and more rapidly, lengthening his phrases from three words at a time to seven or eight.

By one in the morning he had said the entire prayer one hundred times over, but still he could remember only the first line. Try as he might, both with the old square characters and with the Roman ones, he was unable to bring the remainder before his eyes, nor hear the sounds reverberate in his head. Fleischmann knew from experience how difficult it was to remember sounds for more than a few seconds. His father had been dead only eight years, yet already he had forgotten the sound of his voice. The same would happen with his brother's voice. Even listening to recordings of their voices he would no longer recognize them.

Fleischmann was horrified at the prospect. Even in his present state, deprived of memory, he felt instinctively but obscurely that it was somehow up to him to determine his brother's destiny. He began again to repeat the words of the prayer but the telephone rang. It was his sister-in-law asking him to make her something to eat. She had been keeping watch by her husband's bedside and was by now completely exhausted. Her sister had relieved her. It wasn't right to leave him alone, poor man. She needed a bath and a bite to eat. She would be around in twenty minutes.

'Twenty minutes . . . twenty minutes . . .' he repeated to himself. Perhaps if they had left him alone he might have succeeded in learning the rest of the prayer in the remaining hours of the night, but if it went on like this . . . But then how could he deny his sister-in-law comfort?

'Fine, come on round,' he said, and went to wake the housekeeper. Then, before going to help her prepare a hot meal, he shut himself in his study and tried to see whether the interruption had helped make room in his head for a few words of an unknown language. He attempted a quick self-hypnosis, but he was too agitated to use it to help him remember. So he transcribed the text of the prayer into the memory of his personal computer. 'Perhaps tomorrow, reading it over and over on the screen in front of my eyes, I'll learn it. I'll get up at five. No, at half past four.'

His sister-in-law wept copiously, her tears falling into the soup-bowl before her on the table. Long after she had locked herself in the bathroom, Dr Fleischmann could hear her cries. She seemed to be talking to someone, shouting and railing at him, but in the sort of blubbered secret language that schoolchildren use. It frightened him.

As a child he too used to have conversations, before going to sleep, with someone to whom he spoke only in rhyming verse; and he would ask him every night to let him die together with the rest of his family, all at exactly the same moment, so that none would suffer pain at the death of the others. How long was it since those conversations had ceased? 'What a mess we get ourselves into!' he said all of a sudden, and locked himself in his study.

He spent hours in front of his computer. Until dawn the low hum of the screen was accompanied by a quiet muttering. With first light there was silence. At seven in the morning his housekeeper saw him leave the room.

'I've learned it,' the doctor said. He woke his sister-in-law, who was huddled up on the sofa, with a kiss on the forehead; he took her home for a change of clothes, and together they set out in a taxi for the old cemetery in Kozma Street.

His brother had been washed and dressed and was lying in the simplest of coffins in the House of Purification. His face was a luminous yellow. The terracotta shards placed on his eyes and on his lips made Fleischmann think of a new-born child.

The Purifier of Bodies Goldstein whispered in the cold of the room: 'It took four of us to get him ready. There are four of us. Four, do you understand?' He was looking for an appropriate reward. And as if to demonstrate his own honesty he pulled a wrist-watch out of his pocket. 'Take it. And this was his ring.'

The effrontery of this piece of theatre distracted Fleischmann from his spasmodic repetition of the prayer for the dead. He gave Goldstein some money, took the objects rescued from an untimely burial, and gave them to his sister-in-law. He unbuttoned his coat, then buttoned it up again; he rubbed his frozen hands together. The Purifier asked him to go outside. Fleischmann turned to say goodbye to his brother in his coffin. 'I bought the grave for both of us,' he murmured as he left.

After the speeches, the tears and the thunderous prayers, the congregation moved towards the grave. Fleischmann had managed, by paying an appropriate sum, to secure a site near the entrance, away from the older and more overgrown area. A small crowd had gathered, around 200 people.

The coffin was resting on two planks of wood above the grave. Doctor Fleischmann's heart was beating fast. The time had come for him to recite the prayer. Someone gently took hold of his arm. He felt a great tension in his chest and in his throat. With a huge effort of will he spoke the first part of the prayer, at the top of his voice, almost shouting it. He had won. The words emerged clearly and distinctly from his mouth. He, Abraham Fleischmann, was affirming the meaning of the world, of life, beyond all doubt and bitterness. He had to do it for his brother.

He opened his mouth to shout, even louder than before, the second phrase of the prayer for the dead. But with a feeling of terror he realized that he could no longer remember the sounds. The letters themselves had been wiped from his memory and he stood gawping, his mouth wide open. The graveyard was silent. Everyone was looking at him. Fleischmann was sure that his brother was watching him from the coffin. But the second phrase would not come to him. He could only remember one word, one that contained all the vowels, and the mysterious sound of that single word howled around inside his head. Someone understood his embarrassment and spoke the second phrase in his place.

'There, now for the third,' he thought. 'Yes, there's that word that reminds me of a dog, yes, like a command to attack. But what might it mean? What is the meaning of that word? I must have someone translate the prayer for me. Maybe then I'll remember it. But no, the meaning doesn't count. It is so vague. It's the form that matters. And it's that—the sounds—that I don't remember any more.'

Someone, meanwhile, was finishing the prayer in a monotonous, sing-song voice, speaking quickly and without reverence. Fleischmann wanted to cling to this word or that as they surfaced from the waves which rose in the lungs of the speaker and headed inexorably towards him.

And then suddenly there was silence. 'Can the prayer have been that short? And I couldn't learn it!'

Someone passed him a shovel. He had to throw the first clod of earth. He bent over, scooped up some earth in the shovel, and threw it on the coffin which had been lowered on ropes into the grave. He heard a thud. It was the sound of the only good deed he had managed to do for his brother.

As he felt himself being shaken by the hand and kissed on the cheeks, Doctor Fleischmann was still trying to evoke the words that he'd found and then lost again.

He returned to work without a period of mourning. What was the point? He had to think of his patients, he had to try to help the living since he was unable to help the dead.

And yet every morning after shaving he spent a quarter of an hour repeating the prayer to himself. He brought to bear all the techniques he had learned in the preceding weeks. He used every mental trick he knew, exploited all his psychological skills. He tried to imagine idyllic countryside scenes; he concentrated on regular breathing; he repeated words that were supposed to be able to overcome the guard of what we call consciousness. When he missed a word, he would look at the book. In the evening before going to bed he would switch on the screen, plug in the keyboard and start up the computer for a couple of runs through his act of faith, the prayer for the dead.

After two weeks of this he put himself to the test. Everything went well up to half-way through, but his memory of the second part was very poor. He was missing crucial words. Doctor Fleischmann was taking ten minutes over a prayer that could be spoken in forty seconds.

A t the hospital he started to work with a will. His patients seemed on their way to recovery; he saw hope for all of them. He continued to repeat to himself the prayer for the dead, but each time he got stuck at the same point, after which he could remember no more. Still he felt he was making progress.

One evening he went to bed exhausted after a long series of visits. He fell asleep and immediately began to dream. In the dream there was the solemn air of a momentous event. He was in a beautiful room; his brother entered, looking healthy, elegant, a little awkward the way he had always been, and stopped in front of him. He reached out towards the doctor, incredibly happy and benevolent; then laid his hand on his shoulder and began to recite word for word the prayer for the dead. He smiled as he pronounced the meaningless syllables. But this time it seemed to the doctor, quite unexpectedly, that he understood their meaning. There was no need to translate the words into this or that language; they had a sense—inexplicable, unrepeatable—in themselves.

Fleischmann kissed his brother's hands as he serenely continued his psalmody. And then something else became clear: all the childish meanings that the doctor had attributed to the words—because of the resemblance of some sounds to those of words he knew—really were there; his often obscene associations seemed to coexist happily with the true and solemn meanings and they cheered his spirits.

When his brother had finished saying the last word of the prayer, Doctor Fleischmann said to himself in his dream: 'At last I've learned the whole thing. For it was I who was reciting the prayer. My brother is a figure in my dream. So I can't be ill. The worst of the sentences that nature can pass, the biochemical disturbances by which fats paralyse and obscure our blood vessels, count for nothing. For man exists beyond memory, beyond language and meaning.' He was already half awake when he finished this sentence.

He opened his eyes and saw the grey light of early morning. His feeling of joy evaporated instantly. 'What if it really was my brother who said the prayer from start to finish? Perhaps he really did visit me, who knows how, who knows from where?'

After those of the prayer, other words began to disappear slowly from Doctor Fleischmann's vocabulary. Faces and shapes disappeared from his sight, melodies from his hearing. Towards the end his memory had almost completely deserted him. When they took him in to St John's Hospital, he didn't remember ever having had a brother. To Isaac Rosenwasser, who together with a nurse helped him into the ambulance, he said: 'Everything is written in the white spaces between one letter and the next. The rest doesn't matter.' Left among the appointments and scientific observations on the back of an instruction sheet for the use of his computer, was the following scrawl: 'The louder you shout, the better he'll hear you.'

Translated from the Italian by Piers Spence

For the complete works of Abraham Fleischmann, see *Nuova Vita*, nos 1, 2, 3, 4, 1970.

MARKÉTA LUSKAČOVÁ
MOTHERS, DAUGHTERS,
SONS

1986. Belfast.

1986. Belfast.

1978. Whitley Bay, Tyne and Wear.

1965. Jrhoviště, Czechoslovakia.
Opposite: 1975. Cheshire Street, East London.

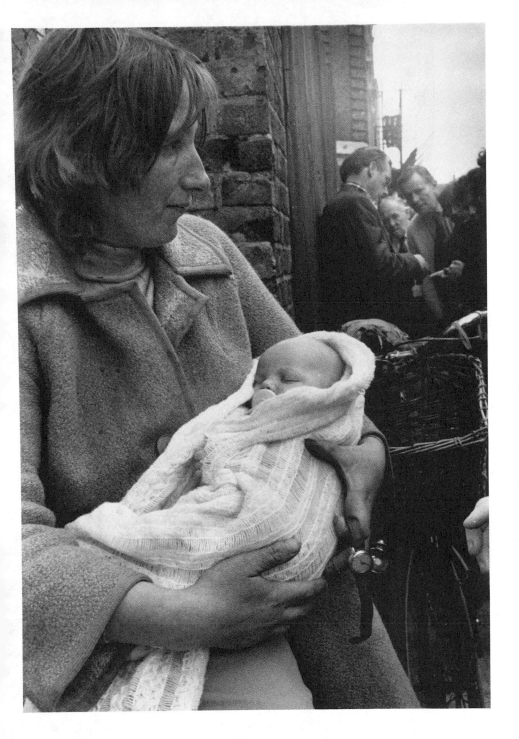

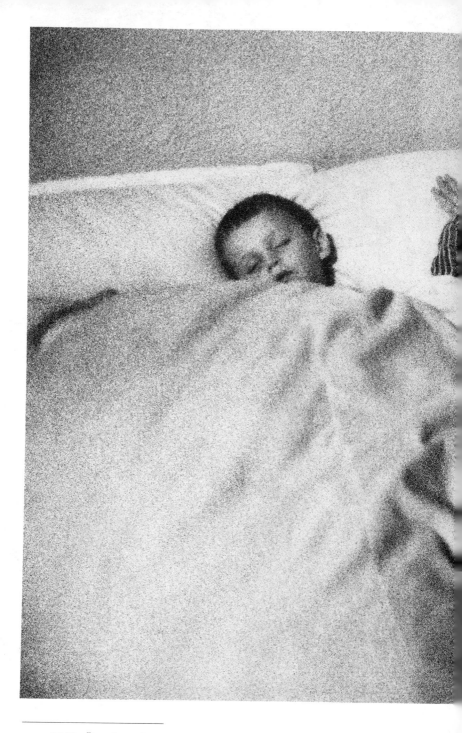

1968. Šumiac, Czechoslovakia.

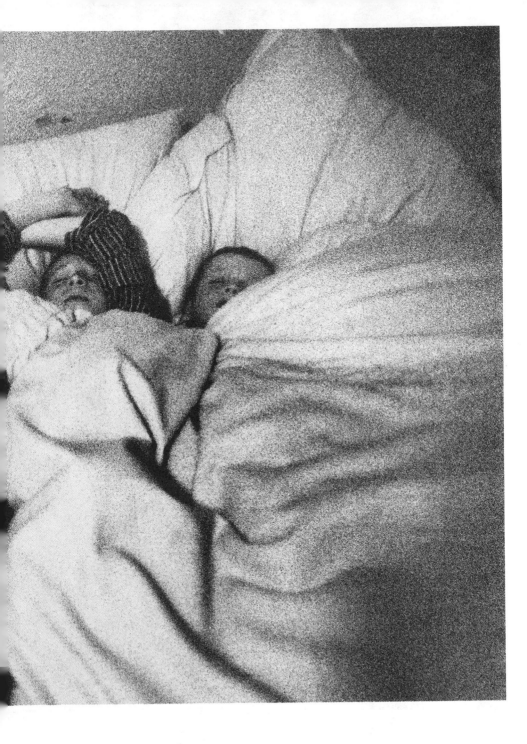

1977. Home for battered wives, Chiswick, London.

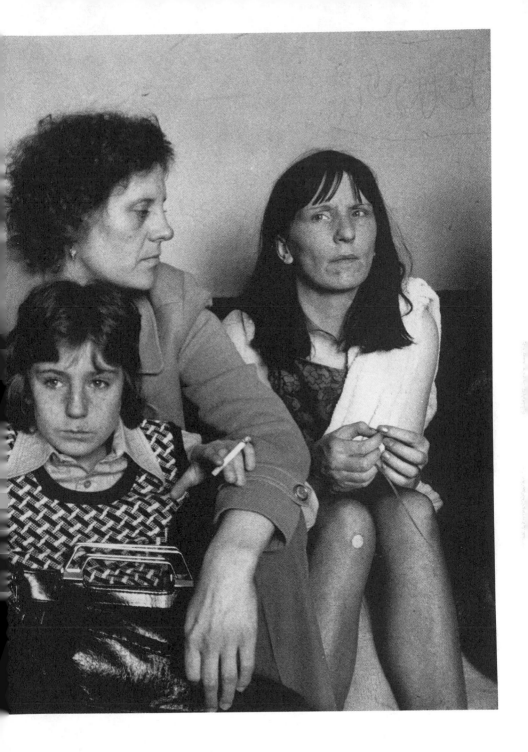

1976. Brick Lane, East London.

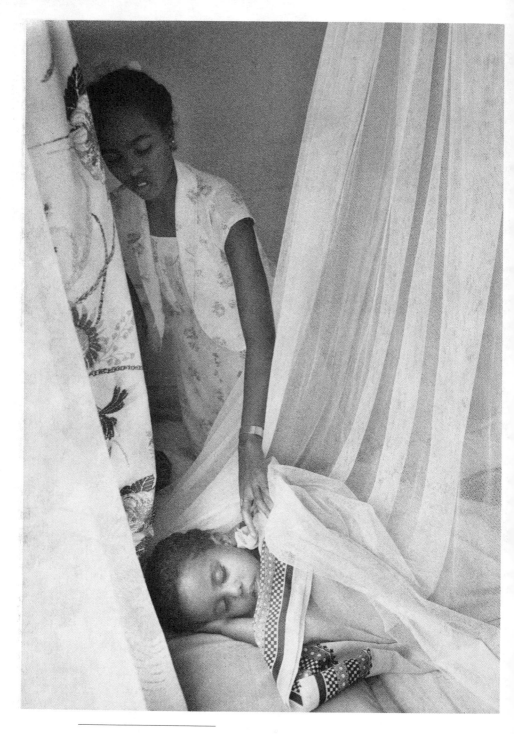

1987. Kenya.

1976 Brick Lane, London.

1979. Sclater Street, East London.

1978. Cullercoats, Tyne and Wear.

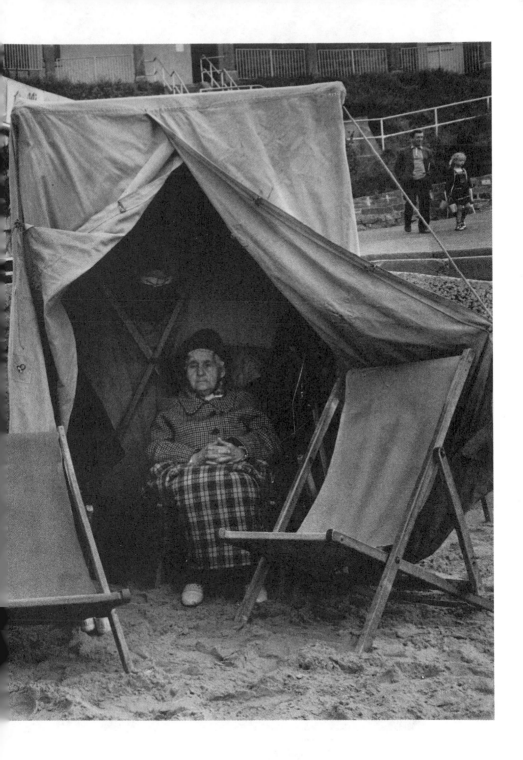

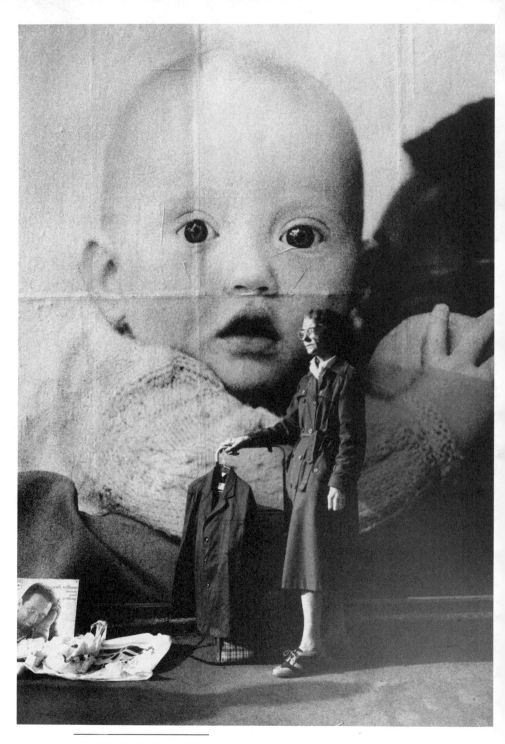

1990. Bethnal Green, London.

GEOFFREY WOLFF
WATERWAY

One May afternoon, at the end of Nicholas Wolff's junior year at college, aboard our boat, *Blackwing*, drinking beer so cold we needed mittens to hold the cans, reaching rail-down into the sun and towards the beach at Mackerel Cove on the New England island where we live, Nicholas and I struck a deal: on graduating from Bowdoin, Nicholas would take this boat to the Bahamas with one or two chums.

There was nothing to it: other than taking full responsibility for our boat which *I* pay for, and teaching his friends to sail, navigate, cook on a galley stove without blowing up the galley, other than maintaining the sails and gear and engine and electronics, and troubling that the dinghy wasn't stolen, and earning enough money before he sailed from home to keep himself afloat without work for six months, and making certain the anchor didn't drag when autumn and winter gales blasted him, and learning first aid, and keeping his friends out of the ocean and clear of the boom . . . Why, there was nothing to the venture but a nod, a wink, another beer and a far-away look on Nicholas's face that I took to be gratitude for my trust, but was in truth cogitation.

During the following year, when friends would remark what a generous fellow I was and how trusting (how could I bank on a mere boy with so much boat? wasn't he grateful?), that circumspect countenance would steal on Nicholas's face, and he'd catch my eye, and I'd shrug. In fact, I had every reason to trust him: he was handy; he didn't get seasick; he knew (as I didn't and don't) celestial navigation; he'd been trained to strip down and repair a diesel engine; he'd sailed offshore weeks at a time on a tall ship; he'd been aloft in great seas and screaming winds; his instincts on the water seemed flawless. We'd been together on the water since he was ten, and in trouble he had never failed to come through.

Besides, *Blackwing* would either winter over in my back yard (while I paid the bank and watched her cradled in blocks,

---

Opposite: Geoffrey and Priscilla Wolff aboard their boat, *Blackwing,* in the Bahamas.

swathed in tarps and crusted with snow a few yards from a blue spruce) or in the Bahamas. Which would she prefer?

He got her there. He and two college buddies provisioned her and prepared her for sea in September, while hurricane Hugo made its way up the east coast from the Caribbean. When it passed, Nicholas gave them a crash course in the rudiments of sailing, and slipped our Jamestown, Rhode Island, mooring the first day of October: Block Island, Fishers Island, the Thimbles, Long Island, City Island, the East River, Sandy Hook, Manasquan, Atlantic City, Cape May, Chesapeake City, Sassafras River, Annapolis, Smith Island, Norfolk, the Dismal Swamp, Elizabeth City, the Alligator River, Ocrakoke, Oriental, Beaufort, Wrightsville Beach, Waccamaw River, Charleston, another Beaufort, New Teakettle Creek, St Simon's Island, St Augustine, Daytona, Cocoa Beach, Vero Beach, Fort Pierce, Palm Beach, Fort Lauderdale, Key Biscayne, the Gulf Stream, Gun Cay, the Bahama Banks, Chub Cay, Nassau, Allan's Cay, Hawksbill Cay, Sampson Cay, Pipe Creek, Staniel Cay, Georgetown, Eleuthera, Governor's Harbour, the End Of The Road.

That road was six months unwinding, bristling with pitfalls and Sirens and drug dealers and drug agents and anxiety and shoals and snags and reefs and the worst gear-busting winter winds ever recorded in the southern Bahamas.

Priscilla and I had agreed to meet our son and our boat at Governor's Harbour on the hundred-mile-long island of Eleuthera on 20 March. Such rendezvous are laughably quixotic. On our end we had flu to avoid, blizzards to pray against, semi-tropical airlines with semi-tropical attitudes toward confirmed reservations and clockwork schedules. On Nicholas's end was a complex of nautical machinery, his body's machinery, weather systems, kismet.

On 20 March, we landed at Eleuthera's little airport and took a taxi to the harbour. In the harbour, swinging from a mooring thousands of miles from home, were our boat and our son. The boat was impeccable, the sun shining, the son tan and grinning.

With what mixed feelings Nicholas surrendered command of *Blackwing* might be imagined. With what mixed feelings I took responsibility for safely returning Priscilla, the boat and me to Rhode Island might be imagined. The idea was to take it easy, to laze 300 miles through the islands of the northern Bahamas and back across the Gulf Stream; then to push about 1,000 miles up the Waterway to Norfolk; then to bring her the final 600 miles home, reading the seabag-full of paperbacks we'd brought, catching some good rays, watching the handsome world float by at five miles per hour—less, if we wanted to hang out. I had finished and revised a book; Priscilla was on leave from teaching. We felt we deserved this, and we knew we needed a jolt to our routine. Back home we were owned by a house and trees and gardens and processes of maintenance that had become habitual. We were past due for a sea change.

During the transition week we stayed in Eleuthera at a friend's beach-house. Most mornings that week Nicholas instructed me an inch at a time in the foibles of the boat I had taught him to sail. The boat looked different. It looked better. It had always looked good, I think, but Nicholas had made it look better. He had finished *Blackwing*'s cherry interior bright, laying up coat after coat of varnish. (And where did three six-footers sleep while the varnish was drying?) Above decks he had taken all the brightworked teak down to bare wood, and brushed on eight coats. Below, the bilge was dry, smelled sweet. The sails had been cleaned and spot-mended. You would not guess looking into my son's bedroom at home that *Blackwing*'s ice box would have been scrubbed, but it had been scrubbed.

He had made our boat sound and clean, and made us happy. There was nothing more that he could do, except sail with us twenty miles north up the west coast of Eleuthera to Hatchet Bay, and say goodbye.

The day we sailed, as all Eleutheran days so far, was clear; the wind was fair; *Blackwing* moved fast through twenty-five feet of water. We could see the bottom; we disciplined ourselves not to look down. We instead stared ahead, trying to make out distinguishing features along what seemed to be an undifferentiated coast. There are no navigational aids in the 'Bahamas'—a corruption of the Spanish *baja mar*, low sea.

In less time than it takes to tell, we were sailing through a hole in the wall, and making our way to a mooring of the Hatchet Bay Yacht Club. A few feet from the mooring pickup Nicholas said the water looked to him 'thin', and I was on the point of requiring him to define his terms when I ran us aground in soft mud.

I don't run aground. Ask anyone. Maybe I *used to* run aground, in Chesapeake Bay, but I DO NOT RUN AGROUND.

'Dad, we're high and dry. Tide'll ease you off in a couple hours. Mix a Mount Gay and juice. Be mellow in the islands, mon. Gotta blaze, Ma. I've got a plane to catch.'

There was water enough to float the dinghy, and I rowed my son ashore, and asked him how often this had happened to him.

'Well, that's a weird thing. Never, actually.'

(Well, actually: would *you* believe him?)

ENTRANCE TO HATCHET BAY

2

After Nicholas said goodbye, Priscilla and I had a long, hard look at our hole cards. Neither told the other, then, but both wondered, what did we think we were doing? After Priscilla reminded me of our agreement, that (after we crossed the Gulf Stream) she could jump ship whenever she was fed up with *Blackwing* or its crew, we decided to feel laid-back. We put a Zoot Sims tape on the deck, were pleased to have verifiable corroboration that a rising tide floats all ships, ate a fine meal.

The harbour was snug and pretty, bordered by the little settlement of Alice Town.

This Saturday night a volleyball game was being played under arc lights against a neighbour from the archipelago now called the Family Islands. It was a sweet occasion: we could hear bellows of enthusiasm, and Priscilla and I smiled a private smile, happy to share (at a little distance) the Bahamians' childlike pleasures, to hear their boisterous huzzahs.

The next morning, in transit to Royal Island, trying with what would become comic inefficiency to get a weather forecast, we heard a news report. Dozens of people injured last night during a fracas at half-time of a volleyball match in Alice Town. A mêlée. Bottles had been thrown, police and ambulances sent for. How the world seems is not how the world is.

At Royal Island we anchored in a palm-fringed lagoon that resembled a movie set of Eden: water as clear as crystal, abandoned plantation, coconut palms backlit by a Tintoretto sunset, soft evening. Sixteen boats were anchored in the large, nearly land-locked harbour; the moon rose, showing its sharp-edged silver face like a cheerful, goofy neighbour peering over a fence, *hey guys, what's cooking?* The nautical almanac had said the moon would rise and it was so, the spheres in their regulated cycles, time and tide right with the world. As the night lavished softness, the moon spilling such unpolluted light that we could see by its beams our anchor dug into the chalky white sand below our keel, and as the breeze piped up we heard the voices of wine and beer and rum drinkers float across the water, singing the songs sung in the back of school buses ('Roll Me Over'), and around camp-fires ('Row Row Row Your Boat'), and by God we joined in. Was this OK or what?

We were gathered into the anything-goes euphoria of strangers sharing a discovery. Then it got rowdy, as though the whole harbour were drunk on liberty. Someone shot off a parachute flare and we heard chivvying gasps: Bad Form. This Is Not Done. Flares were reserved for Mayday emergencies, to signal grave distress. To set off a flare back where we thought of as *back home* would bring the Coast Guard down on a mariner. Back home, playing with flares was much deplored; horsing around with flares, a rum job, a hanging offence back home. But we weren't back home. For sure. So another boat lofted a parachute flare, and another, and soon the lagoon was bathed in moonlight, starlight, phosphorus. Phosphorus in the velvet water, phosphorus aloft. The harbour was lit and so were we.

I went below, and spread out the charts. Again. I'd been studying the ungiving things since the night we met Nicholas in Governor's Harbour and, to my disenchantment, they weren't more inviting tonight than a week ago. The problem was simple: to get to Little Harbour in the Abacos, the northernmost Bahamas chain, we had to navigate more than fifty miles (fifty-three, to be precise, which is what I had to be) of Northeast Providence Channel. To sail the reef-strewn Bahamas at night was unthinkable, so we had ten hours from dawn (seven a.m.) till sundown. *Blackwing* could do five and a half knots under power in calm seas and neutral current. We had to hit Little Harbour Bar on the button. I spent the next several hours calculating courses and tidal sets.

If the wind (or tidal current) was on *Blackwing*'s nose, we wouldn't make it. On the other hand, if the wind was behind us, or abeam of us, we probably would, unless something went wrong. Moreover, if we *almost* made it, there was no escape hatch, no harbour of refuge. We'd cross a line of no return five hours out from Royal Island, and if we went for Little Harbour, and the wind clocked around on us, coming to blow against us, we were out of luck.

The rum was beginning to wear off. I had shut down Jimmy Buffet for the night, and was playing a tape of Pablo Casals doing Bach solos. He was working his way through a threnodic patch, and I explained to Priscilla that I was 'apprehensive'.

She cocked her head at me.

I said I was 'anxious'.

She asked me what I was talking about.

I said it was going to be a 'tricky' passage. Maybe 'chancy'. Not 'tranquil'. In fact, I was looking at alternate routes back to the coast of Florida. An easy passage would take us home by

THE NORTHERN BAHAMAS

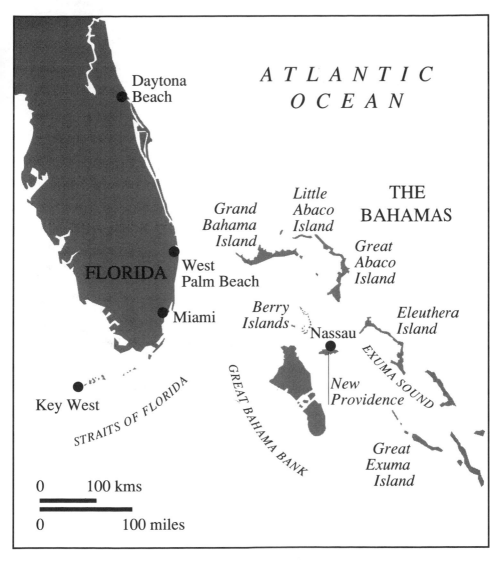

way of Nassau and Freeport, shit-holes.

Priscilla said she'd hang her head in shame. When it came down to it, Priscilla seemed always to be the one of us who put the thing in gear, and stepped on the gas. She likes to know the pros and cons, but I'm not sure why; it takes a lot of cons to turn her off course.

So next morning we got our hangovers out of our berth an hour before dawn. While Priscilla made peanut butter sandwiches with Ritz crackers, and packed them in Ziploc bags, I tried to tune in Charley's Locker on the transistor radio. In the Bahamas, on weekdays, at six forty-five a.m., maybe, if reception was good, it was possible to tune in Charley's Locker from Coral Gables, Florida, to get a rough prophecy of weather in the Caribbean. This followed a round-up of sports news from Trinidad and Jamaica, and was preceded by a maddening hornpipe shanty, 'Barnacle Bill the Sailor' or the like. The velocity of Charley's weather report was remarkable; someone was paying by the second. It was possible, if the boat was pointed in just the right direction, and if the seas were quiet, and wind wasn't shrieking in the rigging, and Priscilla remembered not to talk while I listened, and I kept alert despite a numbing chatter of cricket scores, to hear every third or fourth word in the only experience in the Bahamas (other than trouble) that befell us fast. I tuned in Charley, and he sort of seemed to bring passably OK news. Windsouthwest-somethingknots-somethingelse-by afternoon.

'Let's go,' I said.

It was a hairy passage.

We jumped off at the first hint of light, got up in oilskins and wool caps and gloves. The wind was up and at 'em, twenty knots at first, gusting to twenty-five. The day was grey and ominous, with low clouds scudding in from the west-south-west. The rusted wreck of a fertilizer freighter was the last vessel we saw that day. We were headed due north into great cresting rollers; but as the wind increased, spindrift blew off the tops of the surge, spraying us with warm water. When a gust hit, it came from the west. The wind was beginning to clock around, and I was tense, racing the sun to cross Little Harbour Bar before dark, and safely.

Priscilla noted loran fixes—read from an electronic position calculator—and nautical miles accumulated on the log and kept me equipped with hot tea and peanut-buttered crackers. I hadn't eaten peanut-buttered crackers since I was a kid, and neither had Priscilla; she re-invented them for this voyage and this is why she's so smart: she knew that a quantity of those crackers, dry in zip-locked bags, would give our windswept, water-soaked cockpit a milk-and-crackers-at-recess comfyness. This passage was a trial for her. All these years she'd fought seasickness, and now we were trying a timed-release drug taken by way of a patch worn behind her ear, and either it was working, or she was too busy hanging on and helping out to be sick. That was the good news. The bad news: I was working hard to keep *Blackwing* on course in those wilful seas, with the wind building and coming more and more off her beam. Plus: beginning just after noon, past the line of no return, we could see lightning on the horizon, and hear thunder. Plus: the steering felt sloppy, and I heard the rudder creak when I adjusted it to counter the violent push of a roller on our port stern quarter.

There is no worse destiny in heavy seas than to lose a rudder (other than being stove in, or catching fire). Nicholas had had a steering cable break a few weeks ago, while cruising in the Exumas, navigating a tricky reef. He'd been sailing with a flotilla of friends, and they'd provided him with a spare cable after he'd managed by skill (and maybe luck) to get out of trouble But now the cables would be impossible to replace or adjust. I had an emergency tiller, but it would take all my strength to keep *Blackwing* on course with it, and I was cold and tired. I felt short-handed; I *was* short-handed, and I elected to keep my anxieties about our steering system to myself.

A simple truth we couldn't ignore: Priscilla—smart, brave and calm—is not strong. She has an unerring sense of place, so that she could thread us through a reef. She would cheerfully go below and make food in wild seas. She kept a running record of our time and probably location by the process known as dead reckoning. But to ask her to douse and furl a sail in huge seas, or to trim a sheet, or to wrestle the wheel out here where all was too big for our britches—this was to ask too much. Unspoken between us was a contract: I sail, she thinks. Her will wasn't in question, or her nerve; she was overpowered, and I wasn't, quite. But there was only one of me (alas, alas!), and that one was now wearing out.

The thunder and lightning hit us with full force at four in the afternoon, just after we'd caught sight of a landfall on Great Abaco. When the rain hit us in wind-driven horizontal sheets, we could see nothing but grey wet and evil electric bolts, and the concussive thunder scared us silly. I wondered to myself what it would be like, if I couldn't find Little Harbour Bar, to ride this out at sea, through the night, waiting for dawn, hoping to find my way across. Wondering this, I heard Priscilla say, 'that's it'. The 'it' to which she referred was a reef, forbiddingly named The Boilers, a mile or so south of the bar. If 'it' wasn't 'it', all bets were off, and we'd rolled snake eyes. Time was short now. But 'it' *was* 'it', and now all that remained was to follow the *Yachtsman's Guide to the Bahamas*, which Priscilla read to me above the scream of the wind and the thunder and the smash of the sea.

> Little Harbour Bar should be negotiated with care, according to the following directions. Approaching Little Harbour Bar from the south, stand off the coast not less than one mile until Little Harbour Point and Tom Curry's Point are in transit. (See sketch chart of Little Harbour.) They will then be bearing roughly 305°. Alter course to port to keep them on this bearing until in mid-channel between the point and the line of breakers on the reef that extends south from Lynyard Cay. Then alter course to north, running parallel to the land for about 400 yards, in order to clear the reef that extends for about 300 yards north from Little Harbour Point. You will then be in 18-24 feet. As you alter course, rounding the reef to the port, a cove behind the lighthouse will open up. This will be easily recognized by the white sand beach and a group of coconut palms in the eastern corner. This is not a good anchorage.

See what I mean? Clear as mud? If you don't see what I

mean, if you see instead what the *Yachtsman's Guide* shows, if you see it with utmost clarity so that you could put a hand on *Blackwing*'s wheel, and guide her over the reef, then you're of Priscilla's tribe. 'Look,' she said. 'Look there!'

I looked, terrified what I might see. It was a pretty beach, our anchorage, which was a very good anchorage. A pink sand beach. And over it, arched from way out at sea, near the ungodly depths called The Tongue of the Ocean, to the spot off Lynyard Cay where we dropped anchor, a rainbow.

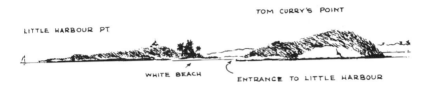

I thought of it as her rainbow, and do. When I met Priscilla in 1963 she was temperamentally unlike anyone I'd known; I fell in love with her for the inexpressible reasons people fall in love but also for a character I can try to articulate, her unimpeded clarity of vision and expression. Of course Priscilla had understood the *Yachtsman's Guide*, and of course she had translated its dense instructions into a rational course of action. If I couldn't have counted on Priscilla to continue to see and say unambiguously, we wouldn't have come to this place in this way. Imagine someone who sees things and systems whole, and who says precisely what she thinks. Not that she says whatever she thinks: she says only what she thinks. Such a person can neither be fooled nor fool, and to live with her is to live with the recurring surprise of hearing a sane consciousness expressed with insanely serene candour. It is frightening to be wholly understood; it is bracing; it is fun; it keeps me off reefs. Because Priscilla's relentless good sense has no interest in prudence, because her comprehension is a renewable resource driven by curiosity, because to see the world through her eyes is to see a misbegotten human comedy rather than a blighted human tragedy, because she said something crossing Little Harbour Bar

233

that made me laugh, because I associate her with light—warmth and buoyancy and illumination—that was her rainbow, and is.

It is worth feeling wet and cold to feel dry and warm. It is worth being scared to be secure. It is worth leaving sight of land to make a landfall. More than a few times, *Blackwing* had been an instrument of instruction in these truisms, but to be safe aboard her, with Priscilla, in the lee of those very reefs that caused such dread, was to feel the kind of gratitude that it is irrational to feel for inanimate objects. Perhaps this was why Priscilla—bringing a tray of rum drinks and cheese to the cockpit—found me below in the engine compartment, tightening the steering cable. It had been well secured and abundantly greased by Nicholas, but it had stretched, as new cable will, under the strain put on it today.

'Come on out of there,' Priscilla said. 'The sun's setting.'

'I know,' I said. 'I need the last of the light to adjust her steering.'

I saw Priscilla make that ancient sign of schoolyard and marriage, eyes rolled upward while forefinger circles ear clockwise.

'What's the matter with you?' she said. 'What's wrong with tomorrow?'

The question was sensible, as far as it went. It failed merely to accommodate how I'd feel tonight leaving undone what ought to be done to thank our boat for bringing us safely to this place, the rainbowed and sundowned glow of which I was missing to thank our boat for bringing us to this place. Well, it confused me, too.

3

Last night we'd seen through our open hatch the stars clear and sharp in the flawless atmosphere—Arcturus, Spico, Regulus, the Southern Cross—and the next morning came in clean and bracing. Studying the charts, planning our complicated passage from Lynyard Cay to Marsh Harbour (the metropolis of the

Abacos) to Hope Town, I noticed over the tops of my sunglasses an inflatable dinghy, pushed by an outboard, grinding towards us. The irritating noise (irritating when someone else was making it but not when I was making it, when it was *necessary* and *up-and-about* noise) reminded me how quiet was the world here in these Out Islands. We were anchored off a pretty beach—down here we were always, when we were anchored, anchored off a pretty beach—not a boat or person in sight, except this one, nearing from Little Harbour. It was churlish to resent company; call me churlish. Here he came: 'Ahoy, *Blackwing*! Where's the Cap?'

'I'm the captain. And owner.'

'Oh.' The fellow bobbing alongside, a little more or less my age, was disappointed. 'Where's Nick?'

This question would be repeated all the way home: *where's Nick?* To meet returning north the people he had met migrating south was an odd sensation. He'd made many friends, and these were not the friends I predicted he'd meet. The water south to the Bahamas is so well-ploughed by yachts that the Inland Waterway is sometimes called the Blue Flag Expressway, for the blue flags flown from boats whose owners are not aboard. I had predicted that Nicholas and his friends would meet the paid hands of boats much bigger than *Blackwing*, crews of young men and women not much older than Nicholas. In fact, the boys of *Blackwing* preferred the company of people like us, oldsters looking for an adventure, middle-class couples (with an occasional remittance man or woman thrown in to raise the tone of the venture) who had cashed in their chips, sold the pencil factory or software patent or house in Shaker Heights, to quit the world and wander.

It was an oddity of many of these people that they brought with them vestigial Polonius- or headmaster-inspired wisdoms, so that many felt compelled, especially after a dinner served on their boat, to clear their throats over a glass of brandy and ask Nicholas and his friends when they were going to settle down, get with the programme, start on their careers. They evidently detected no irony here. They may have been provoked to counsel by Nicholas's vague version of his recent history and his plans. He was less than forthcoming with newly met friends about the title to *Blackwing*; when asked who owned her, he knew he couldn't say he did, or he'd be mistaken for a drug dealer or—worse!—a rich kid. He also wouldn't confess the plain fact, *my daddy let me have the keys*. So he'd take on a cryptic mien, shrug, look at the night sky, say *some guy in Jamestown asked us to bring her south*.

We met dozens, scores, of people along our way who told of kindnesses done them by our son and his friends (without telling us of the kindnesses they returned). We heard stories of Nicholas's ingenuity with tools, his eagerness to lend a hand, his seamanship, his curiosity, his friendliness.

The fellow in the dinghy, a long way from home in Tulsa, declined our invitation to come aboard. He said to tell Nick he'd really done it this time.

'This one's worse than Wax Cay Cut; he'll know what I'm talking about. We screwed the pooch this time.'

What happened: the sailor and his wife had bounced across the bar of Little Harbour lagoon at high tide of a full moon. Now they'd have to wait for the next full moon to bounce back out.

Sailing the southern Abacos was a trial of attention. To sail is to attend: in New England the eye strains to pick out a buoy or the loom of a light. Here we watched the sea's surface for the tell-tale ripples of a shifting wind, and studied the sky for its lessons and warnings. But now we looked down as well as up; it is said of the Bahamas' shoals that the most valuable skill a navigator can bring to their successful circumvention is an aptitude to 'read' the water. By this is meant an ability to distinguish between the dark blue of deeps, the turquoise and aquamarine of adequate depth, the green of a grassy bottom, the milky pale yellow of sandy shoals, the white of a sandbar dry at low tide, the dark patch that looks like coral but is only a shadow cast by a cloud, the brown of coral that can tear a hole in a boat's bottom (not to be confused with the harmless brown of 'fish muds', caused by bottom-feeders eating dinner, stirring up the marl). Nicholas, who is colour-blind, nevertheless learned to read the water from *Blackwing*'s bowsprit, or in especially perilous waters from up her mast. The downside of that upside, he told us, was a clear view of sharks working the bottoms.

Learning to read thin water is an incremental adequacy; the apt scholar of shoals depends not only on memory and common sense, but on sunlight from above and behind. Sailing into the sun it is impossible to differentiate between the shades along the sea's spectrum. So we had to plan our passages, which demanded snaky course changes through erratic channels, according to the sun's declination, which often warred with felicitous tides. We trained ourselves to disregard our terror, to pretend to know better, to smile as we sailed into what seemed to be five feet, four, two. But I'd reach the end of an Abacos passage, strike the sails, line up a casuarina with a church steeple, triangulate that line with a line bearing 287° to the butt of a dirt road, dodge a sandbar, home in on a watertower (looking sharp for the submerged pilings of a wrecked pier), drop the anchor and uncramp my white-knuckled hand from the wheel and a dumb unfelt grin from my face.

But what if the worst had happened, if we'd been holed up for a week or two in one Eden in place of another? Or the other worst: we had had to spend a night at sea, floating two and a half miles above the bottom of Northeast Providence Channel? After all, I wasn't a single-handed Joshua Slocum dodging growlers, icebergs and pirates in the Roaring Forties. I wasn't commanding a convoy escort on the Murmansk run. Seen from above we must have made a dandy picture, sailing like gangbusters through pristine water under a warming sun. This was the Bahamas, as in the Sunday newspaper supplement ads. And if my keel hit sand? *Blackwing* would float off on a rising tide. And if she didn't? We'd wade ashore and phone Allstate.

As these verities sunk in, we settled into what became (for a time) a tranquil routine. The sun would wake us; we'd drink coffee and orange juice; we'd laze in the cockpit waiting for the tide to do the right thing. We'd make a shopping list; we'd take the dinghy ashore to search for ice and bread and beer and fruit and cheese; we'd find what we came for. We'd take the dinghy back to *Blackwing* and laze in the cockpit; we'd observe that it sure was a nice day; we'd think aloud that it was almost warm enough to swim; we'd say we were thinking about taking a swim; we'd swim; we'd sit in the cockpit, letting the warm air dry us; we'd notice it was coming on towards the lunch hour; we'd discuss lunch; we'd make lunch; we'd eat lunch; we'd say we were considering a little nap; we'd take a little nap; we'd pull up anchor and sail a few hours to the next pretty beach; we'd drop anchor; we'd make rum drinks; we'd take the dinghy ashore for a dinner of fried or sautéed or grilled grouper or flounder; we'd bring the dinghy back to the *Blackwing*; we'd put a tape in the deck, maybe Dave McKenna, maybe Thelonius Monk; we'd sit in the cockpit, looking at the night sky; we'd go below to our berth; we'd lie on our backs talking, looking at the night sky. We'd sleep.

4

It was time to get out of the Abacos and across the Gulf Stream to Florida. North of Green Turtle Cay casual yacht traffic thins almost to vanishing, except for liveaboards transiting from north of Palm Beach into the Bahamas in the late fall and early winter, and back home in the spring. The northern Abacos are mostly uninhabited, with a desolate end-of-the-world atmosphere, especially on a cloudy day during a blustery north-west passage of twenty-five miles, driven by a north-east wind of twenty knots to Allan's-Pensacola. This was an abandoned Air Force missile tracking station, populated by moray eels in its reefs and barracuda in the mangrove flats. Oh, and sharks. Did I forget to mention sand fleas? Sand fleas weren't a worry when the wind gusted to thirty knots, but anchoring was.

I use a heavy anchor called a plough, made in England by CQR (*secure*: get it?). I swear by it; I swear by anything weighing twenty-five pounds that can arrest the drift of another something weighing 10,000 pounds when that other something is being hammered by a great north wind. The holding power of an anchor is a function of physical properties that can be mathematically calculated, once that anchor is set. To set an anchor—that is an art; I believed it was an art I had mastered.

Priscilla would bring *Blackwing* into the wind under power, and slow her till she was dead in the water, and I would nonchalantly, imperturbably lower the anchor to the bottom (no undignified heaving, no tangling myself in chain); I would then aloofly pay out anchor rope (called *rode*), while *Blackwing* drifted astern. When five times the water depth had been unflappably paid out in rode (I had marked it in twenty-foot increments), I would snub the rode to a cleat, and observe diffidently how, as usual, the anchor had CQRly bit into the bottom. I would then nod to Priscilla an almost imperceptible nod (no wild oaths, please, no despotic commands, no assholery) to shut the engine down and start chipping ice for the rum drinks. I would sit quietly in the bow, triangulating lines of sight on various objects ashore, casuarinas, say, or maybe palm trees. Meantime I would casually pay out more rode as *Blackwing* drifted astern, till I had achieved the desired ratio of seven to one, rode to depth.

Except at Allan's-Pensacola Cay. We were dressed in oilskins, weary, lonely, wet and cold from the front's spill of rain. It was late in the day, and the sun was too low to light the reefs that ringed both shores of the harbour, the only harbour within reach, a harbour said to be marginal in a northerly. Two boats were anchored close to each other, further up the harbour, where we would like to have been. Priscilla brought *Blackwing* into the wind; I lowered the anchor; *Blackwing* drifted fast astern; the anchor bounced uselessly along the hard-pan sand bottom. I could see it bouncing. It made me angry to see this, and to haul in rode and chain and twenty-five pound plough also made me angry, and made me reflect on how lucky was Priscilla to have in her hands a varnished teak steering-wheel instead of a muddy length of chain. This process was repeated for the next hour or so: the helmsperson, following the anchorperson's despotic commands, manoeuvred *Blackwing* into the wind; the anchorperson lowered the anchor, which skipped along the hard-pan bottom, provoking from the anchorperson wild oaths.

This routine did not proceed in solitude, unobserved. To watch a couple anchor a boat is one of the sea's great amusements, way more entertaining than a world-class sunset or moonbeams filtered through casuarinas. It is proof of one's

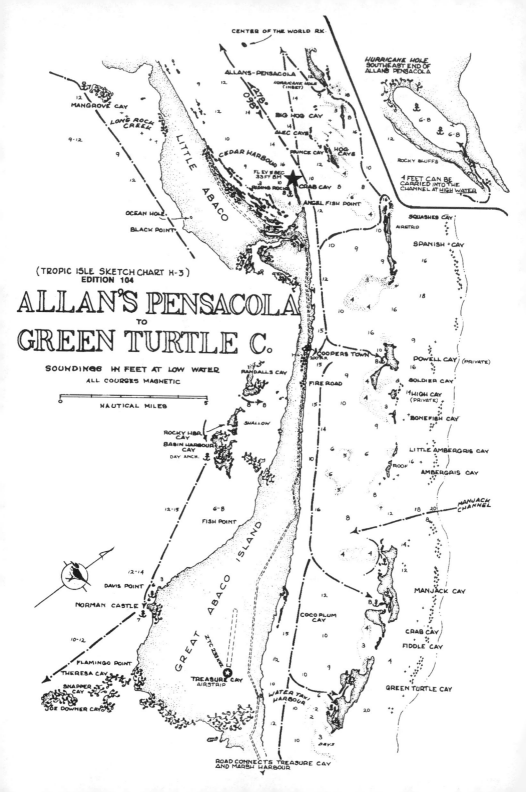

superiority to observe—from the CQRity of one's own steady state, with one's own vessel tugging fruitlessly at what holds it, with a beverage cooling one's hand and perhaps a dish of beernuts nearby on one's cockpit table—a couple less evolved hurling oath, command and anchor. The world at such a moment is starkly binary, split between the anchored and the would-be anchored. Up at the head of the harbour were two boats, one of the anchored was pretending not very successfully to be not watching us. He was smoking a pipe! This pipe-smoking shook me to my rubber wellingtons. It was not right. And then, as though that were not enough, the pipe-smoker turned towards *Blackwing*, languidly, and motioned *my* helmsperson, to whom *I* gave despotic orders, to approach. And then, as though that weren't enough, she did his bidding.

'Holding's bad down there,' said the skipper of *Inshallah*, a heathen corruption of *que será, será*. 'Anchor here, between us.'

Priscilla commanded me, tyrannically, to lower the anchor, and I did, and it held. There was marginally room enough for our three boats to swing, if they swung together, without hitting. The skipper of *Inshallah* had violated a first principle of the Law of First Anchored: he had welcomed us to his sanctuary. This generosity was a breach of all anchoring protocols. I didn't know what to say, so I sulked. Priscilla said, 'Thank you.'

The skipper pulled on his pipe, which he smoked upside-down. 'I'd dive on that anchor,' he said. 'To make sure it's set.'

To examine an anchor in the Bahamas was always advised, because in the clear shoals it was an easy chore, sometimes even fun. (No one dives into Block Island's New Harbour to counterfeit study of his anchor dug into mud and beer cans and shit.) I eyed the mangroves seventy yards from my bow, and mused on the barracuda feeding there, in competition with sharks. I wondered whether the little food fish that lived among mangroves ever toured seventy yards to sightsee a plough anchor, and whether the bigger diners followed them on such a safari.

'You think it's a good idea to dive on that anchor?' I said.

'Well, I do think it's a good idea,' said the master of *Inshallah*.

'I think it's a good idea,' Priscilla said.

'You want to dive on that anchor?' I asked Priscilla.

Priscilla looked at me; she cocked her head; she shook her head slowly. I had a hunch she was thinking about where she was spending her sabbatical, and with whom.

'What I think I'm going to do,' I said to Priscilla and to her pipe-smoking friend on *Inshallah*, 'I think I'm going to slip down there in the water and have a look at that anchor.'

So I did. The water was warmer than the air, and the wind was blissfully uninteresting below the troubled surface. I stayed down there, looking sharp for predators, glancing behind toward the reefs and eels. A dozen feet down the anchor rested on rather than in the bottom; its flukes were tangled in a furze of eel grass, and each time the wind blew *Blackwing* astern, the rode went taut, and the flukes strained at the grass, and held. I dove, and laboured to dig the flukes into the bottom, and it was like trying to dig them into the surface of a parking lot. So I tangled them thoroughly in the grass, and broke the surface gasping, and told Priscilla and her best friend that I wasn't all that impressed by what I'd seen. I didn't want to lean too hard on this, because night was coming on, and I couldn't imagine anything I less desired than to raise anchor, go elsewhere and try again. This was weak of me, and imprudent, and in violation of all maritime usage and decorum, but I was of a mind to say *what the hell*, to say, as it were, *inshallah*.

Our neighbour pulled at his pipe and remarked that he had been in this very spot four days, diving among fish, and he sure hadn't dragged. 'I'm dug in so deep I'll have to blast my way out.'

I would have responded with appropriate awe, but his other neighbour, his friend, had just arrived at *Inshallah* for cocktails, having rowed a little dink into what was now a thirty-knot gale.

That night, all night, while the wind gave *Blackwing* a battering, shaking her mast, rattling her rigging, bringing her to the end of her anchor rode with a jarring shudder, I stood anchor watch. I didn't have fun. I wished I'd never examined the anchor on the bottom; faith thrives on blindness. I had lit an anchor light, in deference to doctrine, so we wouldn't be run down by anyone coming on Allan's-Pensacola by night, which of course nobody would. Our nearby neighbours also showed anchor lights, and a few hours after midnight I saw *Inshallah* move to leeward, further and further astern. I watched, and wondered what to do. The pipe-smoking, among-man-eating-fish-diving, anchor-dug-in skipper surely knew what he was doing; he was no doubt paying out more anchor rode. He was not; he was dragging down on the reef, and as soon as I realized this, his neighbour began to shout and to blow a fog-horn at his friend. The skipper of *Inshallah* was standing at his bow. No, that was the skipper's wife; the skipper was rowing his anchor and chain back upwind. It was an extraordinary feat, and he got it done, and got his anchor down in time, and did not lose his boat on the reef. No thanks to me. I made a mental note: next time you see an anchor light move, holler, the way Nicholas would.

5

Tomorrow dawned. We crossed a Gulf Stream as untroubled as a goldfish pond. Piece of cake. There was no confusion about the boundary of the Stream. If the unlikely transparency of Bahamian reef water is a hundred feet, the Gulf Stream allows visibility of three hundred; it is a warm (eighty degrees) river rushing north from the Yucatán Channel, gathering speed from the Coriolis force and from prevailing winds, bottle-necked between Florida and Bimini, crowded with sea creatures. I remembered reading the observation of a *National Geographic* photographer whose dives had been frustrated by sharks: 'When man enters the Gulf Stream, he enters the food chain. And he doesn't enter at the top.'

Our worry—and we had to have a worry or it wouldn't have been a day on the water—was being pushed so far north by the Gulf Stream that we couldn't make (or *lay*, as navigators say) Palm Beach. To take the effect of the current into account, I had charted a vector course, pointing our nose way south of Palm Beach in order to be crabbed north, and hit Lake Worth Inlet on the money, which is the only thing you can hit if you hit Palm Beach. The accuracy of this vector course depended entirely on a constant speed forward through the water. If something slowed or stopped us, we'd miss our landfall.

I was the alpha wolf in a pack of three fools; the other two boats depended on the accuracy of my loran readouts, and on my navigational shrewdness. One skipper decided he didn't believe we had to point so far south, and so he veered off my course, heading closer to the rhumb line (straight line, loxodrome, least distance between two points); he drifted north of Palm Beach and was last seen bobbing towards Labrador. (We were in radio contact until he declared he was resigned to his destiny; *inshallah*.)

There was lightning on the western horizon, but I didn't care about lightning. I cared about the United States Coast Guard. Let me tell you, sailing in the Gulf Stream is like sailing into a war zone. Coast Guard vessels were evident at all points of the compass. I mean big ships, ghostly white, with anti-aircraft batteries, and machine-guns and cannons. My dread was to be approached, stopped, boarded and searched. Not that I was running cocaine or weed or guns or—bank on it—money: if we were boarded near the axis of the Gulf Stream we'd be driven north at six nautical miles per hour, and that would make us sad. *Blackwing* is black (which is why she's a *Blackwing* rather than a *Redwing* or a *Snowball* or a *Flamingo*); a black boat is a red light to a white boat. I tried to make us inconspicuous, nonchalant; I did this by looking casually in the direction of the Coast Guard vessels—on the theory that they'd be suspicious if we pretended not to notice them—and by talking to Priscilla about poetry. I assumed they could hear us through their directional microphones, and I'd never heard drug dealers discuss poetry with Sonny and Rico on *Miami Vice*. I deduced that it was a mark of drug dealers that poetry was one thing they did not discuss. Live-aboard sailors had ascribed to the Coast Guard and DEA uncanny deductive powers, and I hoped that the Coast Guard had deduced that drug runners would on no account discuss poetry while running drugs across the axis of the Gulf Stream.

We'd been boarded and searched leaving Governor's

Harbour by the Royal Bahamas Defence Force. Half a dozen uniformed men bearing automatic weapons had materialized in a fast inflatable runabout. They'd made a thorough search, opened a few tins of food, studied the bilges, looked through our duffelbags. This had been courteous; the enlisted men had joked with Nicholas about the Boston Celtics; when they left, the officer in charge had wished us *bon voyage*. Courtly, but with locked and loaded fire-power at port arms.

We knew we were watched. Unmarked planes flew frequently and low over our anchorages; it was conventional wisdom that the blimps we saw every day were equipped with high-resolution cameras of the kind used in satellites, and that if we were questioned by the Coast Guard where we had cruised, it was best to remember exactly, since the Feds had our itinerary thumbtacked to their bulletin board. Drug stories shouldered aside a more human-scale island mythology. We wanted to hear sweet stories, funny stories, instead we were warned about yachties being shot or burned to the water-line for poking a bow into the wrong cove, and we were told of hijackings and unsolved murders and beatings.

We would stand four-square against the drug scourge, but pretty please not along the axis of the Gulf Stream. In the event, we were left in peace until we were coming through Lake Worth Inlet in a thunderstorm, zero visibility, and a Coast Guard patrol boat radioed us and the other boat in our mini-convoy (the third having been set a little north of Greenland by now). We were naughty: we had entered the territorial waters of the United States of America without flying a quarantine flag, which is a little yellow triangle beseeching the Coast Guard to come aboard and rummage for contraband. Nicholas had warned us to fly that flag, and now the Coast Guard was cross with us even before we'd touched home plate.

Life is a crapshoot: the Coast Guard decided to search one rather than both of us. In the rain. And the wind. Under thunder. And lightning. Half an hour before night. The pointer pointed to our companion. *¡Adiós amigos!* We were out of there. Home. Home?

Come what came, we were safe. Snugged down below, drinking tea, we felt as smug as Magellans. We'd mounted a snapshot of Nicholas and his friends just above the loran readout to remind us of three substantial reasons why we were where we were.

Priscilla was reading Nicholas's log of his passage down the Intercoastal Waterway, a 1,100 mile sequence of rivers, lakes, bays, and land cuts vulgarly titled The Ditch, an inland waterway (protected from the Atlantic mostly by barrier islands) from Norfolk, Virginia to Miami. We were eighty-three statute miles north of north of Miami, at Mile 1017. Powering at five knots (the Waterway is too narrow and tortuous most places to sail), we had 200 hours of travel ahead of us. And that was just to Virginia. Beyond Virginia lay Chesapeake Bay, Delaware Bay, the New Jersey Coast, the East River, Long Island Sound, Fishers Island Sound, Block Island Sound.

It was raining hard now, and I'd lit the kerosene lamp to give us some light and warmth. *Blackwing* has a fireplace, a wood-burning stove that extends the cruising season in New England, but here in Florida a candle cut the damp cold. I liked being below. I thought we'd feathered our nest quite well, thank you. Our house is a rambling Victorian, too big for us, with spare rooms and redundant outbuildings; the place is stuffed with stuff: book cartons that haven't been opened since the mid-sixties, tools and machines to maintain the yard, closets of clothes held like Confederate war bonds in a profitless speculation that they might make a comeback (bell-bottoms, wide ties, white flannels); I've stored variant versions of manuscripts, students' short stories and essays and grades; I've stored empty shoeboxes in case they might be useful for storing something smaller than empty shoeboxes. You know; who doesn't know? But down here, below on *Blackwing*, the concept *necessary* was subject to ruthless revision. What I brought aboard, Priscilla would trip over; things stood trial for their lives. It was comfortable, and comforting, to strip down, to experience what could be lost in a burglary or foreclosure without diminishing us. As the weeks had passed, we had cleaned up our act, and we had learned the acrobatic tricks that made it possible to move with a show of practised grace from the forward vee-berth (as big and as comfy as a queen-sized bed), through the main cabin (with opposing settees, a drop-leaf table between them, a small galley aft on the port side), to the head (tucked tight behind the companionway steps, and under the cockpit's bridge deck). The main cabin was white and clean, with varnished cherry doors and trim, a varnished teak and holly cabin sole, plenty of light. We knew the inches and dark corners of the place we lived, and cleaned what was dirty, fixed what was broken, polished what was dull. Most of Nicholas's friends on the Waterway and in the islands lived aboard bigger and more complicated boats: clunky, over-rigged forty- and fifty-foot ketches equipped with generators to drive the electric refrigerator and freezer (we used block ice), to heat water (we used a kettle), to power the pressure water system (we pumped). Their boats slept six or eight, and four in comfort. *Blackwing* had four berths, but two of us made a crowd. Our boat was simple, and within the tiny universe we inhabited on *Blackwing* we had the experience rather than the dream of control and competence and— sometimes, now, protected from the driving rain—perfection.

We'd expected, living days and weeks in close quarters, that we'd get on each other's nerves. Nicholas had confessed to feeling cramped and corked, and so had his crew. Three had made a good number of friends to share confinement; one could always break off from two to brood, or sulk, or silently scream at the a) inconsideration, b) incompetence, c) imperfect hygiene of the other two, who would not notice, or could pretend not to notice, the absence of the other. Pretty soon the surly one, the tired one, the furious one would pop a cold beer, or tell a joke, or see a funny sight, and the little storm was dead. Now, silent below, watching Priscilla read, no place to go other than the place we had chosen as our comfy prison cell, I wondered how we'd do.

'We'll go right where he went,' Priscilla said. 'It's all here in the log; he'll tell us what to do. It'll be perfect. If we follow where Nick leads, we'll do just fine.'

It was so. He'd been where we were going. Talk about displacement, reversal of customary order. A father says, 'Here are the keys. Drive carefully.' Nicholas, in Governor's Harbour, had said, 'Here are the keys, be careful with the boat.' In fact,

Nicholas's log was more explicitly cautionary than most fathers would dare: a father might say, 'Watch out for speed traps in Connecticut.' Nicholas's log said: 'The chart shows that Green #45 should be left to port northbound; the chart is *wrong*; beware a shoal spot fifty feet northeast of #45.' If we didn't beware, we'd hit it, and that was a fact. There were encouragements, too: 'Went to old hotel near Cocoa Beach Bridge and had a few. Funky joint, like hotel in *The Shining*. Check it out, but don't try to write a book there.' It was pure pleasure, taking Nicholas as our guide. I could invoke Beatrice leading Dante through Paradise, but I'll settle for modest scale: it was relaxing to let the son become the father, not to resist this inversion. He had been where I had not been, and he knew what I did not know: where to anchor, what bridge tender would open the draw on request, who grills a good hamburger, where to keep an eye open for otters, or laughs, or beauty. From this place forward, Palm Beach to Jamestown, we were in his hands. How did we feel to follow rather than lead? We felt swell.

HAROLD PINTER
THE NEW
WORLD ORDER

A blindfolded man sitting on a chair. Two men (Des and Lionel) looking at him.

Des: Do you want to know something about this man?

Lionel: What?

Des: He hasn't got any idea at all of what we're going to do to him.

Lionel: He hasn't, no.

Des: He hasn't, no. He hasn't got any idea at all about any one of the number of things that we might do to him.

Lionel: That we will do to him.

Des: That we will.

Pause.

Well, some of them. We'll do some of them.

Lionel: Sometimes we do all of them.

Des: That can be counter-productive.

Lionel: Bollocks.

They study the man. He is still.

Des: But anyway here he is, here he is sitting here, and he hasn't the faintest idea of what we might do to him.

Lionel: Well, he probably has the *faintest* idea.

Des: A faint idea, yes. Possibly.

Des bends over the man.

Have you? What do you say?

He straightens.

Let's put it this way. He has *little* idea of what we might do to him, of what in fact we are about to do to him.

Lionel: Or his wife. Don't forget his wife. He has little idea of what we're about to do to his wife.

Des: Well, he probably has *some* idea, he's probably got *some* idea. After all, he's read the papers.

Lionel: What papers?

Pause.

Des: You're right there.

Lionel: Who is this cunt anyway? What is he, some kind of peasant—or a lecturer in theology?

Des: He's a lecturer in fucking peasant theology.

Lionel: Is he? What about his wife?

Des: Women don't have theological inclinations.

Lionel: Oh, I don't know. I used to discuss that question with my mother—quite often.

Des: What question?

Lionel: Oh you know, the theological aspirations of the female.

Pause.

Des: What did she say?

Lionel: She said . . .

Des: What?

Pause.

Lionel: I can't remember.

He turns to the man in the chair.

Motherfucker.

Des: Fuckpig.

They walk round the chair.

Lionel: You know what I find really disappointing?

Des: What?

Lionel: The level of ignorance that surrounds us. I mean, this prick here—

Des: You called him a cunt last time.

Lionel: What?

Des: You called him a cunt last time. Now you call him a prick. How many times do I have to tell you? You've got to learn to define your terms and stick to them. You can't call him a cunt in one breath and a prick in the next. The terms are mutually contradictory. You'd lose face in any linguistic discussion group, take my tip.

Lionel: Christ. Would I?

Des: Definitely. And you know what it means to you. You know what language means to you.

Lionel: Yes, I do know.

Des: Yes, you do know. Look at this man here, for example. He's a first-class example. See what I mean? Before he came in here he was a big shot, he never stopped shooting his mouth off, he never stopped questioning received ideas. Now—because he's apprehensive about what's about to happen to him—he's stopped all that, he's got nothing more to say, he's more or less called it a day. I mean once—not too long ago—this man was a man of conviction, wasn't he, a man of principle. Now he's just a prick.

Lionel: Or a cunt.

Des: And we haven't even finished with him. We haven't begun.

Lionel: No, we haven't even finished with him. We haven't even finished with him! Well, we haven't begun.

Des: And there's still his wife to come.

Lionel: That's right. We haven't finished with him. We haven't even begun. And we haven't finished with his wife either.

Des: We haven't even begun.

Lionel puts his hand over his face and sobs.

Des: What are you crying about?

Lionel: I love it. I love it. I love it.

He grasps Des's shoulder.

Look. I have to tell you. I've got to tell you. There's no one else I can tell.

Des: All right. Fine. Go on. What is it? Tell me.

Pause.

Lionel: I feel so pure.

Pause.

Des: Well, you're right. You're right to feel pure. You know why?

Lionel: Why?

Des: Because you're keeping the world clean for democracy.

They look into each other's eyes.

I'm going to shake you by the hand.

Des shakes Lionel's hand. He then gestures to the man in the chair with his thumb.

And so will he . . . *(he looks at his watch)* . . . in about thirty-five minutes.

Notes on Contributors

Mikal Gilmore is a Senior Writer at *Rolling Stone* where he has worked for fifteen years. He is planning to write a book about his family with the title *Shot Through the Heart*. 'Family Album' is drawn from the proposal for that book. Before she died, **Sappho Durrell** wrote reviews for *City Limits* and had almost completed a play based on the life of Emily Brontë. **William Wharton**'s books include *Birdy* and *Dad*. 'Field Burning' is part of a work-in-progress, *Ever After*, which will be published in early 1993. His latest novel, *Last Lovers*, was published in the spring by Granta Books. **Mona Simpson**'s last story for *Granta*, 'Victory Mills', appeared in issue 24, 'Inside Intelligence'. She is the author of *Anywhere But Here*. **Geoffrey Biddle**'s work will be included in an exhibition entitled 'Pleasures and Terrors of Domestic Comfort' which runs in the Museum of Modern Art, New York, from September. A book of his photographs of the Lower East Side, called *Alphabet City*, will be published by the University of California Press in September 1992. **Seamus Deane** is a member of Field Day, a publishing co-operative of writers, poets and dramatists from the Republic of Ireland and Northern Ireland. He has edited *The Field Day Anthology of Irish Writing 550–1990*, the first volume of which will be published in November. 'The Law of the White Spaces' is the title story of **Giorgio Pressburger**'s collection which is published by Granta Books in November. His recollections of the Jewish ghetto in Budapest during World War Two appeared in *Granta* 32, 'History'. **Markéta Luskačová** began taking photographs in 1965. Her picture of the gypsy family on page 206 is one of the first photographs she took. Her photographs of pilgrims at Croagh Patrick Mountain in County Mayo appeared in *Granta* 28, 'Birthday Special!'. **Geoffrey Wolff** is the author of *The Duke of Deception*. His story 'The Great Santa' appeared in *Granta* 34, 'Death of a Harvard Man'. **Harold Pinter**'s plays include *The Caretaker* and *The Birthday Party*.